ZERO KNOWLEDGE, INFINITE TRUST

ELI BEN-SASSON
WITH
NATHAN JEFFAY

ZERO KNOWLEDGE, INFINITE TRUST

THE EVOLUTION AND REVOLUTION OF BLOCKCHAIN TECHNOLOGY

WILEY

Copyright © 2026 by John Wiley & Sons, Inc. All rights reserved, including rights for text and data mining and training of artificial intelligence technologies or similar technologies.

Published by John Wiley & Sons, Inc., Hoboken, New Jersey.

No part of this publication may be reproduced, stored in a retrieval system, or transmitted in any form or by any means, electronic, mechanical, photocopying, recording, scanning, or otherwise, except as permitted under Section 107 or 108 of the 1976 United States Copyright Act, without either the prior written permission of the Publisher, or authorization through payment of the appropriate per-copy fee to the Copyright Clearance Center, Inc., 222 Rosewood Drive, Danvers, MA 01923, (978) 750-8400, fax (978) 750-4470, or on the web at www.copyright.com. Requests to the Publisher for permission should be addressed to the Permissions Department, John Wiley & Sons, Inc., 111 River Street, Hoboken, NJ 07030, (201) 748-6011, fax (201) 748-6008, or online at http://www.wiley.com/go/permission.

The manufacturer's authorized representative according to the EU General Product Safety Regulation is Wiley-VCH GmbH, Boschstr. 12, 69469 Weinheim, Germany, e-mail: Product_Safety@wiley.com.

Trademarks: Wiley and the Wiley logo are trademarks or registered trademarks of John Wiley & Sons, Inc. and/or its affiliates in the United States and other countries and may not be used without written permission. All other trademarks are the property of their respective owners. John Wiley & Sons, Inc. is not associated with any product or vendor mentioned in this book.

Limit of Liability/Disclaimer of Warranty: While the publisher and the authors have used their best efforts in preparing this work, including a review of the content of the work, neither the publisher nor the authors make any representations or warranties with respect to the accuracy or completeness of the contents of this work and specifically disclaim all warranties, including without limitation any implied warranties of merchantability or fitness for a particular purpose. Certain AI systems have been used in the creation of this work. No warranty may be created or extended by sales representatives, written sales materials, or promotional statements for this work. The fact that an organization, website, or product is referred to in this work as a citation and/or potential source of further information does not mean that the publisher and authors endorse the information or services the organization, website, or product may provide or recommendations it may make. This work is sold with the understanding that the publisher is not engaged in rendering professional services. The advice and strategies contained herein may not be suitable for your situation. You should consult with a specialist where appropriate. Further, readers should be aware that websites listed in this work may have changed or disappeared between when this work was written and when it is read. Neither the publisher nor authors shall be liable for any loss of profit or any other commercial damages, including but not limited to special, incidental, consequential, or other damages.

For general information on our other products and services or for technical support, please contact our Customer Care Department within the United States at (800) 762-2974, outside the United States at (317) 572-3993 or fax (317) 572-4002.

Wiley also publishes its books in a variety of electronic formats. Some content that appears in print may not be available in electronic formats. For more information about Wiley products, visit our website at www.wiley.com.

Library of Congress Cataloging-in-Publication Data is Available:

ISBN 9781394373826 (Cloth)
ISBN 9781394373833 (ePDF)
ISBN 9781394373840 (ePUB)

Cover Design: Wiley
Cover Images: © GOLDsquirrel/Getty Images, © Oleksandr Slobodianiuk/Getty Images

Printed and bound by CPI Group (UK) Ltd, Croydon, CR0 4YY

Eli's dedication

To my father, Zami, my staunchest supporter and the one person who has always made me want to accomplish more—and gives me the confidence to do so. To my mother, Yehudit, who continues to teach me grit and patience, integrity and love.

Nathan's dedication

To my father, Bob, the gentlest of men, and an early adopter of world-changing ideas. Revu plu, as he would say in Esperanto. To my mother, Audrey, who built a family so full of people and values—and who, at 81, asked whether blockchain will be massive "in my lifetime."

Disclaimer

No part of this book should be interpreted as investment advice (or anything resembling it).

Contents

Introduction		xi
Chapter 1	Why Blockchain Matters	1
Chapter 2	The Brave New World of Bitcoin	7
Chapter 3	An Overview of Blockchain	17
Chapter 4	Bitcoin's Breakthroughs—and Blockchain's Expansion	27
Chapter 5	Beyond Currency: Blockchain as Infrastructure	37
Chapter 6	Social Media, AI, and the Gig Economy	49
Chapter 7	Roadblocks to Mass Adoption	65
Chapter 8	The Magic of Proofs	71
Chapter 9	Infrastructure for the Unbanked	83
Chapter 10	Blockchain in Practice: Usability, Scaling, and Privacy	89
Chapter 11	Research Springs to Life: From Breakthrough to Blueprint	103

Chapter 12 StarkWare: From Genesis to $8 Billion	117
Chapter 13 The Harshest Critique: Do We Even Need Crypto?	135
Chapter 14 Stablecoins and Meme Coins	141
Chapter 15 The Integrity Web	151
Appendix Questions About STARK Proofs Answered	165
Glossary	179
Notes	183
Acknowledgments	189
About the Authors	193
Index	195

Introduction

In the history books of the future, the rise of the internet won't merit a chapter of its own. True, the world changed entirely when technology suddenly connected billions of people. But the story of the internet will be so intertwined with that of another innovation—blockchain—that they'll be told together as one. Generations to come will neither know nor care where one story ends and the other begins—so much so that the specific terms *internet* and *blockchain* will be virtually forgotten.

Whether you grew up with the internet as a digital native or witnessed its rise, you'll appreciate how it shrunk and connected our world. But human nature is such that we don't pause for long enough to consider that what we've seen so far is just the first chapter of a much bigger story.

Let's consider for a moment how far another world-changing technology—one we all use every day—progressed in the same span of time as the internet.

Electricity was first introduced into factories and homes—for those who could afford it—in the 1880s. It changed everything. Electrification greatly increased efficiency, flexibility, and scale, especially by replacing line-shaft systems. It replaced candles, allowed for later bedtimes; it even boosted people's sex lives—people suddenly had more alone-awake time with their lover.

But electricity in the 1880s was still in its infancy. Four decades later, people would look back and marvel at the naive excitement of an earlier generation. Yes, they had electricity, but it was produced by a patchwork of early power stations that used steam-powered dynamos to supply only the immediate vicinity.

Thomas Edison's Pearl Street Station, which opened in 1882, was able to light up only a few blocks of Manhattan. Power was expensive and used sparingly. By the 1890s, engineers were already transmitting electricity over long distances—most famously from Niagara

Falls to Buffalo, but it was still far from common. It was only in the 1920s that public grids became widespread, bringing reliable power into most urban homes, and gradually, beyond. Electricity was no longer a small-scale local service but a public utility, like water and roads.

Viewed from the 1920s, the new-fangled, handcrafted electricity of four decades earlier would have seemed little short of comical. Likewise, future generations will look back at today's internet and smirk. "So let me get this straight," they'll say. "They built a system that connected everyone in the world, shrunk the universe so you could chat and flirt, buy and sell. But every time you wanted to send money, you had to use the currency of your own country, which was sent to the recipient via a slow relay race of different centralized companies."

"First, they gave their card details to a website—usually by typing in a 16-digit number. Then they punched in a little code on the back of the card, which they were warned never to share . . . except they shared it all the time."

"That triggered a series of transactions through centralized intermediaries, any of which could block the payment. Not only that, the request pinballed from a payment processor to a gateway to the acquiring bank to a card network (Visa/Mastercard), and then all the way back again, with delays and failure points at every junction. That left a lot of people thirsty in Starbucks or trapped at the exit gate of a scorching parking lot, unable to pay."

The conversation is likely to continue with even more incredulity: "The money didn't move right away. It could take days—especially over weekends or holidays. For some reason, banks needed to take a nap, and sometimes froze transactions with little rhyme or reason until they talked to you. And here's the kicker: Everyone in that relay took a fee—sometimes hidden, sometimes not—simply for shuttling digits around." Wasn't the internet already global, instant, and digital? And if the internet itself could function without being under the control of a single company, why was the movement of money so far behind?

Just like the first four decades of electricity seem somewhat quaint looking back today, the first four decades or so of our online existence will soon feel equally primitive. Why? Because today we run our lives via the internet, but pay our way online with money that really isn't internet-appropriate.

Sure, today's digital payments may look like "internet money," but they aren't. Over the course of this book, that distinction—unclear at first—will come into focus.

We don't yet know what our children or grandchildren will call the network now evolving jointly from the internet and blockchain. The future trivia quizmaster will ask about it. We like to suggest the "Integrity Web," and in the coming pages it will become clear why: because this system is not just about moving and storing value. It's also about values, chief among them a value that humanity dearly needs: integrity. We'll argue in the final chapter that this merging of internet and blockchain, which I see as inevitable, will have integrity as its beating heart. That's why I refer to what I'm convinced will become our digital go-to infrastructure of the future as the integrity web.

My path into blockchain was through math—specifically, through the field of cryptographic proofs. That may sound like gobbledygook now, but give it a few chapters. I think it'll start to feel relevant—and maybe even interesting.

The proofs we'll be discussing are minuscule files of data with massive power (the Appendix covers these proofs in technically precise terms). They help verify, organize, and keep honest the vast amounts of information our societies depend on today. It's a branch of math that, in my lifetime, has started to do things once thought impossible. I've had the exhilarating experience of making discoveries in this field—one of which pulled me into blockchain and is now helping shape its future.

Today, our lives run on systems that handle our information and money in ways that would have stunned our great-grandparents, who knew most of the people who managed their affairs. We rely on people in distant offices—or more often, on faceless algorithms. The question we should all be asking is: How do we know we can trust what they're doing?

That's exactly where mathematical proofs come in. The ones I co-invented—called *STARKs*—are at the core of an $8 billion company I helped build. And they do something mind-blowing, which anyone can understand.

Each of us depends on thousands of computations every month. Let's take just one set: your credit card bill. It might contain a hundred lines, each one a separate charge. Are they all added up correctly? Or did someone, through error or malice, sneak in an extra dime? If that happened across enough bills, it would be a quiet but enormous heist.

Let's assume here that your credit card company still sends printed bills. You walk into their printing room, where hundreds of thousands are being prepared. I hand you a small device. It scans the room and flashes green—confirming that every single line, on every single bill, has been added correctly. What's more, the device generates an unforgeable certificate that each customer can use to verify, on their own, that their specific bill is accurate.

That may sound fanciful, but it's not. This is what STARKs are doing—not in the physical mailrooms of credit card companies, but for enormous numbers of digital transactions out in the real world. Anything that requires computation—whether simple additions or far more complex tasks—can be audited this way. STARKs—full name Scalable Transparent ARgument of Knowledge—are the digital equivalent of that mailroom scanner. For context, STARKs are part of a field in math called Zero Knowledge that has advanced rapidly in recent decades—so named because it allows verification without disclosure.

For now, it may feel like I'm telling two different stories: one about blockchain, the other about proofs. But over the coming pages, you'll see how they converge—and how my own path became a story of both. That's also where the two stories come back together. The internet connected us. Blockchain—and the math behind it—helps us trust what that connection is used for. At times in this storytelling, I'll hand the pen to my journalist friend and co-author, Nathan, to help unpack why it matters.

We'll get into the details soon enough. But what matters for now is where all of this is heading. And I'm sure that the answer is toward digital systems that are more private, more efficient, and far more trustworthy. That shift touches everything—from money and identity to how we interact with institutions and with each other.

CHAPTER 1

Why Blockchain Matters

You don't need to be a tech expert or an economist to follow the story that I will be telling in this book, together with my co-author Nathan. You just need to check one of these boxes:

- You have spent money.
- You have owned a document that was important enough that you didn't want it to be corrupted or lost.
- You have some level of curiosity about human beings and how society functions.

Our guess is that you checked all three, so we are good to go. These three themes will be critical to our discussion:

1. *Money*, because that's the best-known function—and today the primary function—of blockchain.
2. *Documents and data*, because blockchain will come to redefine how we handle these and which ones we trust as the "source of truth."
3. *Human beings and human society*, because, in truth, anyone who describes blockchain as just "a technology" or "a money system" really doesn't get it.

A blockchain is a shared digital ledger—a record book that lives online, which is copied across many computers. It is designed so that once something is written into it, nobody can secretly change or erase it. I don't mean they can't do so without penalty—they simply can't. And that's what makes this a story about integrity, not just tech.

So, instead of relying on a government office, religious authority, or corporate database, the blockchain itself becomes the reference point everyone can check. At its core, blockchain is a system that will redefine how we carry out some of our most important interactions with other humans—moving value (money), determining what records are accurate (documents and data), and coordinating at scale (human beings and human society).

What it gives you is not abstract; it's things that matter to all of us.

To anyone who hates the fact that institutions hold disproportionate power, consider this: banks control the record of your money. Governments and corporations control the records that define your identity and rights. AI systems and algorithms determine how we understand the world around us. And it doesn't stop there. Credit-checking agencies act as judge and jury over whether you can sign up for this or that service, based on their collection and interpretation of your records. They ultimately decide whether you are trustworthy, employable, or creditworthy. They may even shape your family's future by deciding whether you should, or should not, merit a mortgage for the home you want to buy.

Blockchain is about rebalancing that power and cutting out this huge web of middlemen that exert so much control. Want to check my creditworthiness? I'll give you access to certain details from my wallet (a digital app for managing assets), and you'll see exactly how I conduct myself.

What blockchain offers is such a unique fit for the deep needs of humanity that its mass adoption is inevitable. But if you're thinking to yourself that you don't yet see this happening, you're right. The blockchain world has so far failed to convey a critical message—why any of this matters and how it could help ordinary people in their daily lives.

The big innovations of the last quarter-century—smartphones, cloud computing, social media, movie streaming, and online banking—all have something very simple in common: their names alone tell you exactly what they do. As a consumer, my reaction is simple: I understand it, I want it, and I get it.

The term *blockchain* perfectly captures the technical beauty of the system, but says nothing about what it does or how it can make a practical difference in our everyday lives. Nobody walks around saying, "I need a block and a chain."

Blockchain may have made it into the dictionary (Merriam-Webster, 2018) and become a buzzword because of hype over Bitcoin prices, but it has yet to persuade the wider global public why it actually matters.

IntegrityLand

If you could rub a lamp, summon a genie, and be granted three wishes, what would you ask for? One catch—you're asking on behalf of all humanity, not just for yourself. After all the obvious asks like solving hunger, ending war, curing cancer, and so on, how about asking for integrity?

Integrity sounds like an abstract concept. Maybe it even sounds pompous. But it's not. It's an attribute we can easily appreciate. Just think of it as the antithesis of Las Vegas. Not the city as it actually is, but the city as it's caricatured in popular culture—the version immortalized in slogans, sitcoms, and cheesy bachelor party montages.

Vegas is a metaphor for a place where you can do what you want, act in ways that violate your own values—and none of it counts. "What happens in Vegas stays in Vegas" has become a cliché. You can make choices you wouldn't make elsewhere and hope they vanish the moment you leave. It's a worldview built on the idea that what's out of sight is out of mind, with no consequences to face.

Vegas is a place where even the most solemn of agreements—marriage—is on the blurred borderline between counting and not counting. In movies, drunken Vegas unions are often quickly dissolved, laughed off by friends and family. In the sitcom *Friends*, after Rachel and Ross marry in Vegas, Phoebe, wide-eyed, asks: "Wait, wait. A wedding in Vegas actually counts?" Monica replies, deadpan: "If you get married in Vegas, you're married everywhere."

Imagine a place that represents the exact opposite of this Vegas caricature—a place you head to when you need to make an agreement you care about. You go there because it's a place where contracts can never be faked or tampered with. A place where payments agreed in a contract are made automatically, without intervention. A place where you can entrust money to someone—say, for investment—knowing that every clause governing its use is clearly set out, with guaranteed, unfakeable, real-time tracking of its whereabouts.

Welcome to IntegrityLand. What happens in IntegrityLand doesn't stay in IntegrityLand. It follows you, everywhere and forever, in a good way. Everything you agreed to sticks like glue. IntegrityLand is governed by a system that's as strong as the rules of nature, such as the force of gravity. If it was agreed upon, it happens, period. You go to IntegrityLand when you need something to count—especially if you're dealing with someone you don't know personally (something more common than ever) or whom you don't trust. Or, most importantly, when interacting with someone who has greater power than you, such as a big corporation or government. When you want it locked in, tamper-proof, no loopholes, no pretending it never happened.

The IntegrityLand we are talking about is, obviously, blockchain. It's a system that everyone uses, but because of that, nobody controls. An environment where the system itself is the adult in the room: keeping receipts, holding everyone to their word, and refusing to forget. That's why, as I mentioned, what I foresee is blockchain and the internet morphing in the future, and my working title for the entity I expect to emerge is the Integrity Web.

A set of unbreakable rules like blockchain would have been handy at any point in human history. But today, it's more than handy; it's a matter of urgency. Let's see why.

The Storage of Your "Stuff"

What "stuff" makes up your life? And where is it stored today, compared to where it would have been stored long ago? This storage problem is, at heart, a documents-and-data problem. Who holds the authoritative record of your life and assets, and who gets to be the "source of truth"?

Take money, for example. Where do you keep it? For the most part, not in a shoe box or in a home safe. Most of your money is on a bank's electronic ledger. They—not you—hold the authoritative record of how much money you have. If they (or more commonly, the state directing them) decide to freeze, misuse, or mismanage your funds, you'll likely find out too late and, almost certainly, with no recourse. That vulnerability is the documents-and-data problem in a nutshell.

How do we address this problem? For starters, a tamper-proof public ledger would change who holds the keys to your records. In brief, blockchain protects your "stuff" by making the record public, verifiable, and tamper-proof—so ownership doesn't depend on trusting any single company or government.

Then there are your electronic files. Perhaps the most personal are your photos and videos—essentially, your memories. Most of us now have far too many for our walls or shelves, so they live on cloud servers, where we have no idea if they're being leaked or misused.

Our social media posts—the closest thing most of us have to diaries today—are handled by companies that also hold huge amounts of our personal information. Your life story is posted online in fragments; your likes, your locations, and your interactions are all being used and monetized every day by the people you trust to preserve them.

Another concrete example of your "stuff" is your credit score—our system's shorthand for your creditworthiness. You cannot establish it yourself; a third party calculates it from data you don't control. You can't see how the score is compiled or contest it with your own evidence. Your word doesn't count.

These are just examples. In each, the takeaway is the same. In the past, we would have looked after this "stuff" ourselves, with a big sturdy lock for which we alone had the key. Today, it's in the hands of others.

Of course, we want to retain all the benefits of electronic life. But do we want to hand over so much control to others, slipping it into their black-box systems with no guaranteed way to see exactly what's happening to it? If there were another way that was just as convenient, we believe almost every human alive would opt to use it.

This is important for many reasons, not least that as every year passes, more and more is happening away from our gaze. Millions of platforms are competing for us to download them to our phones, many of which handle some portion of our finances. The way we imagine digital crime is that criminals will siphon huge sums from our accounts. But we are likely to see (or, even worse, fail to notice) crime that involves cheating in the calculations—in the computation.

If criminals do this, the ledgers of the digital world will fill their pockets, potentially with nobody noticing for days, weeks, months, or even years. After all, would you notice if your payment app was miscalculating your balance by a dollar or two?

And the truth is, traditional audit systems can't keep up. They weren't designed to monitor billions of computations happening in real time across thousands of apps. That's why we need new systems—built from the ground up with integrity in mind. Systems where every result can be cryptographically verified, instantly and automatically, by anyone. Not just faster—but provably trustworthy.

The great British writer C. S. Lewis, who died in 1963, wrote that integrity is "what you do in the dark," a quote often paraphrased as "Integrity is doing the right thing when no one is watching." This is precisely what blockchain provides. We already rely on digital systems for everything. Now we need to improve those systems so that they are truly trustworthy. We've moved our lives online—it's time our systems caught up with the integrity we expect offline. And with blockchain, that integrity doesn't belong to a corporation or government that controls it; it belongs to all of us, collectively. In this sense, we reclaim ownership of both our physical and digital lives.

CHAPTER 2

The Brave New World of Bitcoin

I was at the Bitcoin 2013 conference at the San Jose Convention Center in California, and the scene was anything but conventional.

This was my first crypto event—and it couldn't have been more different from anything I'd experienced before. Until that point, every conference I'd attended had been academic: quiet rooms, polite applause, meticulous slides full of Greek letters, always introduced in full protocol as Professor Eli Ben-Sasson. This? This was a different planet, and the standard form of address was "bro."

There were booths with sports cars and entrepreneurs in T-shirts flanked by supermodels. Some of the folks giving keynotes were being asked for autographs. One guy told me he hadn't slept for 36 hours—he'd driven through the night from Canada just to be there. He was that excited.

The word crypto comes from my field of research, cryptography—drawn from the Greek kryptós, meaning "hidden," and gráphein, "to write." But by the time most people encountered it, the term had already begun to shift, becoming shorthand not for the codes themselves, but for the digital currency they made possible.

The energy was electric: a thousand people, many in hoodies, rather than suits, who truly believed they were reshaping the world. I wasn't alive when Woodstock took place, but this is what I imagine the energy would have been like there.

Some attendees were *cypherpunks*—digital rebels who believed in using tech to shift power away from big institutions and back to individuals. Others spoke about new ways for transferring wealth to the next generation, without relying on banks and nation-states.

Bitcoin was still seen as very off-the-wall. Some talked like libertarians. Some talked like philosophers. Some were evidently more comfortable coding in mom's basement than being around people, so they didn't talk much.

The leading economist Garrick Hileman, in a panel discussion, said he thought that Bitcoin "offers the possibility for a real monetary paradigm shift, which is really exciting." Erik Voorhees, a well-known Bitcoin entrepreneur and early blockchain advocate, gave a presentation entitled "The Role of Bitcoin as Money." I remember him reading from a printed speech, which struck me as very unusual, as almost nobody does that in the math conferences I was used to attending. He articulated the significance of Bitcoin in the financial landscape, stating: "Like the Internet, Bitcoin will change the way people interact and do business around the world." Meanwhile, Andreas M. Antonopoulos, a security expert and educator who would go on to become one of Bitcoin's most compelling public voices, dispelled the idea that this technology was being built solely for a politically minded niche. "This isn't a libertarian currency any more than it's a communist currency," he said.

Ever the academic, I wasn't sure that Bitcoin would be truly disruptive. I could only go on what I had empirically seen so far. But I was blown away by what had been achieved to date. It showed for the first time that cryptography overseen by a bunch of otherwise unconnected people, spread across the globe, could literally do everything a bank could do. It could replicate the functions of a financial institution, do a better job, and do it more securely.

I saw this brave new world that I'd wandered into because it fascinated my math mind, without realizing just how different it would be to all I knew. I tossed the presentation I'd prepared. As I'll explain in a later chapter, I wrote a new one from scratch with only one driving objective—to connect my work to the energy and excitement I saw there. And in the hours after I delivered my speech, the reactions changed the path of my life. The feedback made it clear: the math I'd been working on could solve some of the biggest problems facing blockchain.

A quick reminder at this point that when I use the word blockchain I'm referring to the shared digital ledger—a record book that lives online, which is copied across many computers. And I should mention for context that while today there are many blockchains, at this moment in 2013 there was only one blockchain, which was Bitcoin. Bitcoin was founded as a money-only system, which may leave you wondering how we got to the point today that blockchain is about so much more than money. Stay with me—we'll get to that part of the story soon enough.

The Genesis of Bitcoin

People say that understanding blockchain and crypto is complicated. It's not. Or let's refine that statement. Understanding the granular detail relating to the engineering and operation of virtually anything we use in life is complicated. We still eat bread, even though we're clueless about the chemical process that makes yeast rise; we drive cars, even though the internal combustion engine—or indeed the lithium-ion battery—is a mystery. Likewise, we still use money, even if we can't answer a simple question about monetary systems.

The reason so many people feel lost when it comes to blockchain is that its advocates focus too much on the how and too little on the why. So in this chapter we are going to talk about what Bitcoin has brought to the table that is fresh and interesting. Let's return to that 2013 conference and how it completely recalibrated my life's trajectory. Before that, I had a comfortable tenured job in the ivory towers of academia; suddenly, I was infatuated with a world full of anti-establishment vibes. Up to that moment, I had thought of my research in cryptographic proofs as something elegant but niche. At the conference, I saw the path to take it out of a niche, and make it matter to society. It showed me that the challenge of building trust without centralized power was exactly what my work was designed to solve. That shift didn't happen in a single flash, but the seed was planted.

Bitcoin was still in its early years—just four years old—when the conference took place. It was born, on paper, in late 2008. That was when Satoshi Nakamoto—a genius or a collective of still-unidentified geniuses—released a nine-page white paper. Code—transparent, public, and unchangeable computer code—was to be anointed king the world's money system. Or more precisely, governor. Yes, the proposal was bold: a currency with no central authority and no institution in charge. It sounds revolutionary, but at the same time, it's a very old concept: Gold, too, was a currency with no central authority and no institution in charge.

Back on January 3, 2009, as the global financial crisis was raging, the economic system was flooded with emergency loans and massive asset purchases in the order of a trillion dollars to stem the collapse, and disillusionment toward banks was at its height. Then the Bitcoin software launched, and the first coins were created. That first moment is called the *genesis block* (*Block 0*)—the first page in Bitcoin's new ledger.

That same day, *The Times of London*'s front page read: "Chancellor on brink of second bailout for banks." Satoshi Nakamoto placed that exact headline as a note inside Block 0. It worked as a timestamp and a hint at the crisis backdrop in which Bitcoin was born.

A very short aside. Interestingly, the person or people who came up with Bitcoin—Satoshi—vanished in 2011. Why, and to where, is one of the world's biggest mysteries. But it's poignant that after creating a network that crucially had no single point of failure, Satoshi's disappearance dramatically proved this.

Returning to San Jose, three qualities of Bitcoin grabbed me there, and it's the same three that enthrall me today: broadness, public verifiability, and incentivized integrity.

Broadness: The All-Are-Invited Ideal

What is the closest you'll ever get to your country's money system? A guided tour of the national mint, viewed from glass-ensconced viewing galleries? Maybe. Even our local banks keep us at arm's length, increasingly requiring appointments to visit and making it nearly impossible to get a phone number for your local branch. The biggest step banks have taken to make customers more welcome this century is halting the practice of attaching their pens to chains, as if every customer were a potential pen thief. The message banks send us is clear—we, the bank, run things around here. You should take a ticket and wait for the privilege of talking to us.

Bitcoin doesn't have surly employees telling you to wait in line. Normal people enforce the rules and keep the system running. And the clever part is that they are invited to do so. We call this quality *broadness*—anyone, anywhere, can run the system. All you need is a computer and the will to follow the rules.

There's no dress code. No office hours. If you want to participate, you can. That openness isn't just symbolic—it's what gives the system resilience and reach.

Public Verifiability: Radical Transparency

You can't see what your bank is doing with your money or how they keep your records. As we discussed earlier in the book, Bitcoin works differently: thousands of independent computers ("nodes") keep identical copies of a transaction ledger and validate new entries against the protocol's rules.

And not just for the last 6 or 12 months, like on your banking app. Everyone can check everything, from the very moment of Bitcoin's existence. And it will always be this way—this feature is built into Bitcoin's protocol rules. This quality is formally known as *public verifiability*, and it is indeed radical. It doesn't just mean the information is available in theory, like a Freedom of Information request that requires forms and delays. It means you can verify the entire history yourself. No special permission, no fancy hardware. Just download the software, and check it anytime—even on Christmas Day.

Because many nodes store and cross-check the same ledger, no single party can hide, backdate, or quietly rewrite transactions. This is what the blockchain term *trustless* means: you don't have to trust a bank or any single company—you can verify the entire history yourself, either by using a block explorer or by running your own node.

A simple analogy: Imagine a teacher is running a reward program in class. When the children behave well, they earn points. And when the class reaches 100 points, they get a pizza party. Each time the teacher says, "I'm adding a pizza point," the kids cheer—and many of them keep a tally themselves. The reward is too important to trust to a single person or notebook. Everyone watching, everyone checking—that's verifiability.

Of course, transparency comes with trade-offs: everyone can see everything, including your payments. For many, that's not a feature—it's a flaw. The real aim of Bitcoin's design is public verifiability without compromising privacy. And thanks to cryptographic tools like zero-knowledge proofs—which we'll explore later—we're learning how to achieve that goal.

Incentivized Integrity: Why It Stays Honest

The concept you're about to read—how Bitcoin keeps people honest without a boss or central authority—is one of the most beautiful and mind-blowing ideas in modern systems. I'll give you the simplest version first, then we'll make it visceral with a real-world visit to a mine. A deeper technical dive comes later. For now, here's what you need to know:

What's a block?

A block is like a page in a record book. Every few minutes, Bitcoin collects recent transactions, bundles them into a block, and adds that block to the chain of previous ones—hence the term "blockchain."

Who adds the blocks?

People program their computers to compete for the chance to add the next block. These people are called miners. A computer wins the right to add a block if it's the first to solve a tough mathematical puzzle. The winner gets rewarded in Bitcoin.

Why is this puzzle important?

The puzzle is hard to solve but easy to check. Solving it doesn't unlock any secret—it just proves the miner put in the work. It's like a fairy-tale king who sets a seemingly-impossible task for a suitor—not because the task matters, but because the effort proves commitment. This effort makes it expensive to cheat and shows the system that you've "earned" the right to add a block.

Who checks the blocks?

Every participant in the Bitcoin network—called a node—keeps a full copy of the blockchain and checks every new block against the rules. These include things like "no spending the same Bitcoin twice" and "only valid digital signatures allowed." If a block breaks the rules, it's rejected. So if someone tries to sneak in a fake transaction, the network will catch it and throw it out.

Why does this keep people honest?

Because creating a block isn't free. The person running the computer that solves the puzzle has to spend real money—mostly on electricity—to power their machines. A miner who wins the right to add a block, and who then inserts a fake transaction, will have it rejected by the network. You still have to pay the electricity bill, but you get nothing in return. You've shot yourself in the foot. The system is designed so that cheating is expensive and pointless, while honesty is rewarded.

That's incentivized integrity in its simplest form: honesty is rewarded, and cheating is self-defeating.

It's a bit like flowers and bees: miners pursue rewards, but in doing so, they keep the system honest.

Hundreds of books talk about Bitcoin mining—a term that describes the birthing of each and every Bitcoin—but most give readers no sense of what this actually looks like. So in preparing for this book, Nathan and I took a road trip through rural Oklahoma—a place where Bitcoin is finding a foothold in the economy.

It was a glimpse into the future. We even visited a ranch where the always-shirtless chief explained that all investment comes via Bitcoin, and the future of the place is inextricably linked to digital currencies.

At one point on the tour, we visited a Bitcoin mine. If that conjures up images of pickaxes or headlamps, it's a far cry from that.

Rather, there are rows of shipping containers parked in the middle of nowhere. From the outside, they looked like forgotten cargo. But up close, they roared.

The noise was unbelievable: We both have house-party-throwing teenagers, yet it was probably still the loudest place we've ever been. It sounded like a thousand vacuum cleaners battling a jet engine.

What was happening inside is the key to the story of Bitcoin. The computers weren't just whirring aimlessly—they were competing. Each one was racing to solve a cryptographic puzzle tied to a set of transactions. Solving it first meant you'd won the lottery (we'll explain later why the puzzles are in the picture). Out of all the machines worldwide, yours was the one that cracked the code fastest. And the prize? The right to confirm those transactions, add them to the blockchain, and collect a reward. That's what "mining" really means. It's not digging for gold—it's competing to earn trust, using computation instead of shovels. Not physical effort, but mathematical proof.

The man running the place greeted us in a backwards baseball cap, coffee cup in hand. He got started because he was convinced that such a place was good for the future, good for the local economy, and of course, profitable. He didn't need a Wall Street boardroom or federal charter to launch the operation.

But here's what inspired us, standing there shielding our ears: He's not just some guy in a field asking people to trust him. He's chosen to work inside a system that is strict, mathematical, and incorruptible. There are no paneled boardroom doors that can be closed. Anyone in the world can monitor what is being recorded on Bitcoin's network and check that he is operating honestly. He literally can't fudge the numbers. That's the odd dissonance of the place—so rural and hard to find, yet every iota of work visible globally. Through his work, he helps run a financial network that, even at that moment, was serving people across the world.

It was surreal. Instead of trust being granted to someone in a suit, trust was being earned with machines doing honest work because the system leaves no other option.

That's what struck us most. Out in a dusty field, with nothing but humming machines and a man in a backwards cap, the rules of Bitcoin were fully at work. No central authority, no permission required—just incentives, math, and verifiable honesty powering a global network, which brings us back to the core of how this system stays alive.

This is what makes the system tick. It doesn't rely on trust, morality, or a central authority. Instead, it makes honesty the only profitable strategy. Cheating isn't just discouraged—it's a waste of your own resources. The result is a self-sustaining network where anyone can participate, but only those who follow the rules get rewarded. The system stays alive because the incentives are aligned with integrity.

And of course, this model doesn't just apply to Bitcoin. Today, many other blockchains, including those that are part of my own story as I will discuss later, namely Zcash and Starknet, draw their strength from these same three intertwined qualities. They are broadness (anyone can operate the system), public verifiability (anyone can check that the rules are followed), and incentivized integrity (honest behavior is rewarded, dishonest behavior is punished).

CHAPTER 3

An Overview of Blockchain

I'm the kind of person who skips the blurb at the start of recipes and jumps straight to the action; someone who doesn't read the instruction manual for new appliances (or parenting books for new kids). The same is true of Nathan. So we had mixed feelings about writing a chapter that lays out blockchain basics, step by step, as a kind of mental model for use as you continue through the book. Useful, yes. But it also feels like a bit of an interruption to the narrative.

I can already hear some readers saying, "Finally, the primer we've been waiting for," and others flipping ahead to the next chapter, keeping this one bookmarked as a reference. There's no right or wrong here. Use it as you wish—as a primer now, a reference later, or something to circle back to when the story gets deeper.

What Exactly Is a Blockchain?

I have briefly defined this in the preceding chapters, but here is a bit more detail. At its core, a *blockchain* is a useful infrastructure for recording payments, ownership, or agreements—essentially any situation where trust and accuracy matter. Bitcoin was the first blockchain; today there are many.

Blockchains represent a way for groups of people, whether a handful or millions, to share records and rules without relying on a central authority.

Data is stored in *blocks*—units of information. Each block contains hundreds or thousands of transactions, together with a secure, encrypted reference, like a fingerprint, to the one before it. That, critically, is what creates the *chain*. Once a block is added, it's locked in place, a part of the permanent record. Like something "set in stone," you can't go back and change it.

Who runs a public blockchain? That's the beauty of it. There's no central operator—just a network of independently run computers. When new data arrives, each node—an individual computer in the network—applies a shared set of rules for accepting or rejecting updates known as a consensus protocol to check it and decide where it fits in the history. No meetings, no manual votes, just the automated process called consensus—how the network agrees on what gets added to the chain. We'll look at how it actually works—whether through mining new coins or staking existing coins, meaning locking them up—a bit later.

What they're really doing is checking whether a new block is valid. A block is just a bundle of recent updates—like transactions, records, or messages—that someone is proposing to add to the chain. The consensus mechanism ensures that everyone agrees on whether this block follows the rules. If it does, it gets added. If not, it's rejected. That's consensus—not as a conversation, but as code.

Each block is cryptographically linked to the one before it. This means that each block includes a hash—a short summary generated by a math formula akin to a fingerprint—that uniquely identifies the previous block. If anything in the earlier block changes, the hash won't match. To rewrite history, an attacker would have to replace that block (and all that follows) and get a majority of the network to accept the new version. That's why records are hard—though not impossible—to alter, and that's why blockchains are useful for all kinds of collective, peer-to-peer (P2P) agreements.

Anyone can join a public blockchain and view the data, but there are also private or "permissioned" blockchains made accessible only to approved members; these are outside the scope of this book and can be explored separately.

In short, a public blockchain is a shared ledger of truth. It doesn't require trust in a central figure. Instead, it relies on structured math, cryptography, and a network of computers—not on trust in people, companies, or governments.

Who Participates in a Blockchain Network—and What They Do

A blockchain runs on many nodes that form a network of computers. Each node is operated by someone who has chosen to join the network and to run its software. These participants don't take part in the blockchain as people, exactly—they contribute computing power to help keep it running.

Some nodes simply store a copy of the blockchain and help verify new data. Others package transactions into blocks and try to get the network to accept them. In Bitcoin, and several other blockchains including Zcash, these are called *miners*. They compete by spending electricity on a cryptographic "puzzle"; the first to find a valid solution earns the right to add a block and collects newly minted currency (e.g., Bitcoin or Zcash) plus fees. In *proof of stake systems*, such as modern Ethereum and Starknet, they're called *validators* (often also referred to as *block producers*). No puzzles. Instead, they lock up their coins as collateral (the *stake*). The protocol—the rulebook baked into the software—randomly selects one validator to propose the next block and others to verify and attest it. If they follow the rules, they earn rewards. If they cheat or go offline, some of their stake is taken (i.e., "slashed"). The labels differ, but the role is similar: they help decide what gets added to the chain.

Every node checks new data against the protocol's rules. If something looks wrong—like a transaction that tries to spend money twice—they reject it.

Cheating is costly and likely to fail. In miner-centered networks like Bitcoin and Zcash, you waste an enormous amount of computing power and electricity. In proof of stake systems like Ethereum and Starknet, dishonest validators risk losing their stake or rewards. The system doesn't just make cheating unlikely; by punishing bad actors, it actively incentivizes all nodes to operate with integrity.

Participation means dedicating part of your machine to a larger system. It's not about having an opinion—it's about helping enforce the rules by running code that checks and shares what's true.

How Blockchains Reach Consensus

A blockchain doesn't have a leader, editor, or referee. So how does it decide what's true?

Someone combines the latest transactions (such as the payment of a bill or the signing of a contractual agreement) into a bundle called a *block* and "proposes" that it become part of the blockchain. Then the rest of the network checks it in relation to the rules baked into the software, guided by the principle that "code is law." If the block is deemed to follow the rules, it gets added. If not, it gets excluded, and the proposer will suffer penalties. As mentioned earlier, that shared process of agreement is called *consensus*, and it all functions automatically while node owners work, sleep, and so on.

Different blockchains reach consensus in different ways. Bitcoin uses *proof of work*. This means it's a race between computers to solve a hard, software-defined puzzle: find a number (a *nonce*) that makes the block's *hash* fall below a network target (practically, a hash with lots of leading zeros). The hash, to recall, is a fingerprint of the block's contents—things like recent transactions, timestamps, and a reference to the prior block.

Miners try nonces until one works. This puzzle prevents spam and Sybil attacks (attempts to overwhelm the network by creating many fake identities), gives the network a single agreed-upon ordering of transactions, and makes rewriting history prohibitively expensive.

If you're looking for an analogy, think back to *Charlie and the Chocolate Factory*. Remember Augustus Gloop—the kid whose dad bought up truckloads of chocolate bars to find a golden ticket? Bitcoin and Zcash miners are a bit like that. They don't buy masses of chocolate but rather invest in machinery and electricity to win their "golden ticket," namely Bitcoins or Zcash coins. They budget a large outlay, convinced—just like Gloop's family—that the golden ticket is worth it.

You might be wondering, "Does the biggest or fastest computer always win?" The answer is no. The process works more like a raffle—one where having more computing power gives you more tickets, and more tickets mean a better chance of winning. But even a small miner, with just a few tickets, can still win (just like Charlie was lucky to get his golden ticket).

Whoever wins gets to add the next block to the chain. They're rewarded with newly created Bitcoins or Zcash coins (called the block reward) and the transaction fees from that block. It's not fast, and it uses a lot of energy. But the upside is that it's extremely hard to cheat.

Proof of stake (PoS), used by Ethereum, Starknet, and others, replaces raw computing power with financial commitment—and does so with greater efficiency, finalizing blocks faster and using far less energy. Validators lock up some of their coins—this is their "stake." The protocol then randomly chooses one validator to propose the next block. A group of others are selected to verify and attest that the block is valid.

The proposer earns the biggest share of the reward. Attesters receive smaller payments for signing off. But anyone who cheats—or even just goes offline at the wrong moment—can lose part of their stake. This penalty is called slashing.

The goal is the same as with proof of work: a shared history that no one can fake. But PoS reaches consensus faster and uses far less energy.

Why Blockchain Data Can't Be Changed

Once something is added to a blockchain, it's almost impossible to change it. This is one of blockchain's most important features—and one of the reasons people trust it.

Each block stores not only a set of transactions, but also a digital summary of the block before it, which is as unique as a fingerprint. If anything in the previous block is changed, the fingerprint no longer matches. Your node would suddenly see two competing histories—a *temporary fork*—until the network agrees on one.

Because each block depends on the one before it, changing even a single detail breaks the entire chain. That's nearly impossible.

And because the blockchain lives on thousands of computers, not just one, you'd also have to fool most of them at the same time. That's what makes the data so secure.

Even if someone makes a mistake—like sending funds to the wrong person—they can't just go back and edit the record. Instead, they have to create a new transaction to correct it. The original stays in place. They'll have to request the recipient to send the funds back in a new transaction.

Where Does Cryptocurrency Come In?

A higher price means the reward is more valuable. That attracts more participants, who are willing to invest real resources to compete honestly. It raises the cost of attack and makes the whole system more secure.

So cryptocurrency isn't just digital money; it's what powers the machine—and protects it.

A fact that many have forgotten: The term "crypto" originally refers to cryptography—the math that secures the system—not the currency itself.

What Is a Smart Contract?

A *smart contract* is code that runs on a blockchain. It sets rules and makes sure they're followed—automatically.

It works like this:

If X happens, then do Y. For example, if someone sends money to this smart contract then split it evenly and pay both Alice and Bob. No human has to check. No intermediary is needed. The rules are built in. In this example, Alice and Bob can split any payment they receive equally and fairly between them.

Once a smart contract is added to the blockchain, no one can change it. That means everyone sees the same rules, and no one can cheat.

Smart contracts are what make blockchains more than just databases. They let us build apps, marketplaces, games, and systems where people can trade, share, or vote—without needing to trust each other.

The Concern About Privacy

Integrity through incentives is tricky: It works only if the rules are verifiable, and here there is a problem, which may be causing you to shift uncomfortably in your seat. The basic Bitcoin model of verifiability means radical transparency: a window—nay, a magnifying glass—revealing everything that happened on-chain. With Bitcoin, you have gained a model of trust, but privacy is lost.

We're all smart enough to know that when we say we want accountability, we don't always mean such radical transparency. We don't want the nosy neighbor to look up our salaries. So how do we fix that?

With zero-knowledge proofs, a set of cutting-edge math and cryptography that sound like science fiction and which will be a main topic of the coming chapters.

Zero-knowledge proofs are what I call the "have-your-cake-and-eat-it-too" cryptography. They let you prove a transaction followed the rules—without revealing the details of the transaction itself. For example, you can prove you paid your taxes, without showing your full income or where you spent your money. The proofs make it possible to deliver both transparency and privacy.

Here's the key idea: the system still checks that everything is valid—no cheating, no double-spending—but it doesn't have to know who sent what, to whom, or how much. Rules are enforced, but personal details stay private. It sounds magical, but it's real. It's already here.

And now the story gets personal.

If you're wondering just how big a deal zero-knowledge proofs are in crypto, take this example: one of their most important implementations is Zcash, the privacy-focused cryptocurrency I co-founded before starting StarkWare. Zcash is based on a cryptographic protocol I helped create—Zerocash—and uses a cryptographic primitive (a core building block in math) I contributed to: ZK-SNARKs. It's math that proves all the rules were followed, without revealing any private facts. You get transparency without giving yourself away.

In the fall of 2025, Zcash surged in value by hundreds of percent in just a couple of months. Whether that turns out to be a sign of things to come or just a blip doesn't really matter. The real point is that privacy is a powerful motivator in crypto. People are buying it not just as an investment, but as a statement—that privacy matters.

At the time of writing, the SEC had just hosted a roundtable on privacy-preserving technologies. StarkWare's General Counsel, Katherine Kirkpatrick-Bos, was one of the experts at the table. Zcash is being talked about in Washington and beyond. Privacy is now firmly on the agenda.

Which brings us to what might seem like a contradiction. Blockchain and Bitcoin are built for openness—broad participation, honest incentives. But that doesn't mean privacy has to be sacrificed. In fact, it can be strengthened.

That's the mental shift we need to make. Transparency doesn't have to mean exposure. A well-designed cryptographic system can prove that the rules were followed, that the math adds up, that no one's cheating—all without revealing who did what. The system stays honest. The individual stays private. This isn't a hope—it's already happening.

And yet there's still a cultural reflex that gets in the way. Ask for privacy and people get suspicious. What do you have to hide? But that question flips the burden. In a free society, privacy doesn't need a justification. Intrusion does.

Paying in cash doesn't make you a money launderer. Closing a door to make a phone call doesn't mean you're plotting a crime.

Privacy is about preserving agency, not concealing guilt. And financial privacy is no exception. We shouldn't be alarmed by people who want to transact discreetly. What should worry us is the growing normalcy of a world where every payment is tracked, stored, and scrutinized by default.

The Concern About Scale

Radical transparency and broadness resonate with the values of a free society—the belief in the power and agency of all citizens to see how the blockchain operates and ensure it functions with integrity. But this leads to a second problem, beyond the privacy compromise we just discussed.

Radical transparency means everyone should be able to verify that each and every transaction on the blockchain is being executed correctly. We're not going to sit and read through every transaction, of course. Instead, we'll be using our smartphones, laptops, and home computers to participate in this verification process. And here lies the second problem: scale.

Banks and traditional payment systems give us slick interfaces—apps on our phones, websites on our laptops—but behind the scenes, they rely on massive data centers to process and relay our transactions. Blockchains don't have that. There's no backend infrastructure apart from the devices in our hands. And this means we've hit a cruel trade-off: if we push radical transparency and broad access to their logical conclusion, we must dramatically limit the scale of blockchains. Only then can our devices keep up—verifying everything without overheating or draining all our memory. But if we go this route, blockchains can support only a tiny number of payments.

If we go the other way—allowing for a higher rate of transactions—we gain scale, but at a steep cost: many users will drop out of verifying the blockchain altogether. At the extreme, we end up with a system that's open in theory, but only large financial institutions can afford the hardware to actually track it. We're back where we started: an opaque system that demands blind trust.

But there is a way out. And astonishingly, it's the same have-your-cake-and-eat-it-too math we saw earlier when solving for privacy. Zero-knowledge proofs have another superpower—one that almost seems more improbable than the first. Certain types of ZK proofs can dramatically compress the process of verifying that a blockchain has functioned correctly.

ZK STARKs, which I co-invented, can do something remarkable: they allow you—or anyone on the planet—to verify the math behind an entire year of global financial activity, without redoing the math yourself. In other words, you can check that no one has cheated in even a single transaction underpinning the world's financial system.

STARKs make it possible to confirm that bank transfers, credit card payments, Venmo, Alipay, and more have all been executed correctly—down to the last penny. And the verification of a proof that guarantees all of this? It takes less than a second on your phone.

Realizing that ZK proofs solve both privacy and scalability was the eureka moment I had at that Bitcoin conference. The additional thrill? Realizing I might be the first person in the world to see this. That insight—and the work to make it real—is my own small contribution to the blockchain world. I'll tell you more about it later in the book.

What Is a Layer 2 Blockchain?

As mentioned above, blockchains can get slow and expensive when too many people use them at once. *Layer 2 systems*—often called *L2s*—exist to solve that.

An L2 runs alongside the main blockchain. It handles most of the work—like payments or trades—and sends a summary back to the base chain. This keeps things quick and cheap, without giving up security.

Think of it like a side road easing traffic from the highway. The main chain still holds the record. But the L2 keeps things flowing.

L2s are how blockchains scale. They allow more people to use the system at a lower cost, without relying on intermediaries or compromising security based on math and code instead of trust between people.

CHAPTER 4

Bitcoin's Breakthroughs—and Blockchain's Expansion

In the years since Bitcoin 2013 in San Jose, Bitcoin has gone from a niche curiosity to a household name. What started as a countercultural experiment is now something that global institutions either love or love to hate. But one thing is for sure—they can't ignore it. It's discussed in boardrooms, cursed by some regulators, and debated in parliaments. Sadly, at times it has been a divisive political topic. For example, in the 2024 US elections it was loved by Trump and Republicans and discussed with great suspicion by many Democrats.

I have unwittingly become a central character in the story of blockchain's evolution. Teams around the world are building blockchain applications on "rails" that my team and I have created—some of them performing functions I could never have foreseen. My relationship with these people is unlike any other I've ever experienced. We are collaborators in a decentralized story that is now being written, because blockchain has changed not just what we build, but how we build.

Suppose you've seen press coverage about Bitcoin or blockchain. Most likely, that coverage hasn't focused on cultural change or on any of the foundational ideas we explored earlier—radical transparency, the "everyone-keeps-a-copy" ethos, and incentivized integrity. Instead, headlines fixate on price swings and regulatory squabbles. The deeper story—why these technologies matter—is too often lost.

Six Mind-Blowing Features of Bitcoin

Bitcoin is often talked about like magic internet money—or, as Sheldon Cooper in the sitcom *Big Bang Theory* once put it, "a new online currency that has been developed—it's like actual money except you can't see it, hold it, or spend it on anything." That line was meant as a gag, but it hints at something deeper: Bitcoin isn't just a new way to pay—it's a rethinking of how value, trust, and security can work without banks, governments, or any central authority.

We'll soon explore how blockchain evolved far beyond Bitcoin. But first, it's worth spotlighting what made Bitcoin itself so revolutionary. These aren't technical side notes—they're six core concepts that reshaped the way we think about money, ownership, and the systems we rely on. Understanding them will help make sense of everything that followed:

1. Who is this Satoshi Nakamoto everyone talks about?
2. What's the "double-spend" problem, and how does Bitcoin address it?
3. What exactly is incentivized integrity?
4. What is the "hard cap," and why does it matter?
5. Why is "self-custody" important?
6. Can Bitcoin payments be reversed?

WHO IS THIS SATOSHI NAKAMOTO EVERYONE TALKS ABOUT?

As mentioned in Chapter 2, in 2008, the person—or group of people—who came up with Bitcoin published a white paper under the name Satoshi Nakamoto. Satoshi corresponded profusely on email and various electronic forums, and then after a while, he vanished. No media tour. No interviews. No face. Just code, correspondence, and then silence—ever since a final 2011 email in which it was matter-of-factly stated that Satoshi had moved on to "other things."

Over the years, countless revelations have claimed to expose who Satoshi really was. None have held up. The Australian computer scientist Craig Wright, for instance, declared himself to be Satoshi but was ruled not to be him in a UK court. *Newsweek* famously ran a 2014 cover story naming a retired engineer, Dorian Nakamoto, as the founder of Bitcoin (a claim he flatly denied). That article later drew criticism as an example of sensational journalism. Ultimately, all of these false claims reinforced the point: nobody is revealing publicly who Satoshi is, and chasing that identity has become its own kind of media spectacle.

The Satoshi mystery is part of crypto's folklore. But more than that, it's a kind of allegory. The creator disappeared—and yet the system continued to run. That's the point. Bitcoin doesn't rely on any central figure or authority. It's open-source software, maintained by a decentralized network of users worldwide. There's no CEO. No call center. No "Bitcoin Reserve" Chief Commissioner. No "Forgot password?" link. You don't need permission to use it. And no one can stop you.

THE DOUBLE-SPEND CHALLENGE—AND BITCOIN'S BRILLIANT FIX

The idea of digital money sounds great—until you hit one fundamental problem: how do you stop it from being copied?

Most digital stuff works by duplication. You send someone a file or a photo—you still have your own copy. That's fine for information. But if money worked that way, the system would collapse. Imagine taking a photo of a $100 bill, emailing it to 10 people, and calling each copy real. You've just created $1,000 out of thin air.

That's the core issue known as the double-spend challenge—the risk that someone could spend the same digital coin more than once.

With physical money, this isn't a problem. A coin or a bill exists in one place at a time. If Alice hands Bob a $10 note, she no longer has it. End of story.

But with digital currency, there's nothing physical to hand over. And that creates a trust problem. For decades, the only known fix was to use a central authority—a trusted institution that keeps the official ledger and puts its stamp of authenticity on transactions. Think of a bank, a clearinghouse, or PayPal. They're the referees, deciding what's real and what's not.

Bitcoin changed everything.

Instead of relying on a central referee, Bitcoin uses a shared public ledger—the blockchain—that anyone can read and help maintain. This way, no single party has the power to approve or deny transactions, but everyone can verify them.

Every computer (node) in the network checks every transaction and every block against the same rules. To propose a new block, participants called miners must compete using a process known as proof of work. They invest real-world resources—hardware, electricity, and time—to solve a tough mathematical puzzle. The winner earns the right to propose the next block and claim a reward. But if they try to include a fake or duplicated transaction, the network rejects their block. All that effort goes to waste.

Suppose Anna sends Bitcoin to Wei to buy a car. Then she tries to send the same Bitcoin to Pascal to buy a house. Once the first transaction is recorded in the blockchain, it becomes part of an immutable public history. The second one is invalid. It's trying to spend something that's already been spent.

Could Anna rewrite history? Only if she can build a new version of the blockchain that erases the original transaction—and then convince the network to accept it. That means doing more work than the rest of the network combined. Unless she controls over 50% of all Bitcoin mining power—a so-called 51% attack—she can't pull it off.

That's Bitcoin's breakthrough. It didn't just identify the double-spend problem—it solved it. For the first time ever, the world had a way to track digital ownership without needing a central authority to vouch for it. It made internet money possible—and made cheating practically impossible.

INCENTIVIZED INTEGRITY—DRIVING WITH A SPIKE

We covered the mechanics of incentivized integrity earlier—how miners spend real resources to earn rewards, and how cheating is punished by the system's economic design. What's worth highlighting here is something deeper: why this logic holds even when someone tries to break the system.

Picture driving a car with a steel spike mounted in the center of the steering wheel, aimed straight at your chest. You wouldn't take reckless chances, not because you're virtuous, but because the cost of a mistake would fall on you first.

Would you change lanes on a hunch? Take a corner too fast? Have "just one drink for the road"? Probably not. You'd drive with care, because the first person to get hurt would be you.

That's the intuition behind Bitcoin's inherent honesty. Mining a block costs real money—machines, electricity, hours of your life. If you try to cheat, the network rejects your block and the reward disappears. All that effort is simply burned...wasted.

Could you still pull it off? Only by controlling most of the network's mining power—a coordination problem so large that it defeats the very incentives that make the system valuable in the first place. That's a seriously tall order. Miners are scattered across the globe, all competing—and none of them wants to kill the goose that lays the golden eggs.

So the lesson is simple: in Bitcoin, honesty isn't about virtue. It's about self-interest. The spike is always on the wheel. You can grab it if you want—but you'll be the one who bleeds. This is Satoshi's genius: a system where integrity is the most profitable strategy—incentivized integrity.

And even in the wild scenario where someone does have enough computing power to rewrite a day of history, they'd still lose. Say Bitcoin is trading at $100,000. You reverse transactions and redirect 1,000 BTC to yourself. That's $100 million—on paper. But the moment the attack is spotted (and it will be), Bitcoin's credibility takes a hit. The price crashes. The 1,000 BTC in your wallet is now worth far less. You didn't just steal money—you damaged the system that made the money valuable. Even if an attacker somehow succeeds, the victory destroys its own reward.

This isn't just theory. In 2019, Binance—the world's largest crypto exchange—was hacked for about $40 million. Its CEO, CZ, briefly floated the idea of asking Bitcoin miners to roll back the chain—not to cheat, but to undo a theft. He quickly dropped the idea. Even a justified rollback would have undermined trust in Bitcoin itself. And that loss of credibility would've cost far more than $40 million.

That's the deeper logic Bitcoin locks in: a system where integrity doesn't hinge on trust or authority, but is delivered instead by a system of incentives. Honesty is the profitable strategy, and that is what we call incentivized integrity.

WHAT IS THE "HARD CAP," AND WHY DOES IT MATTER?

How many dollars or yen will there be in a decade? No one really knows. It depends on central banks, political choices, inflation targets, and sometimes geopolitical mood swings. Your government is unlikely to reach into your account and actually take your money—but it can quietly erode its value by printing more of it.

Bitcoin flips this model. It has a hard-coded cap: there will never be more than 21 million coins. And its issuance schedule is publicly visible. It can't be changed casually—or even easily. It would require a broad, global consensus. This makes Bitcoin a form of digital scarcity, with built-in resistance to inflation. So Bitcoin is closer to gold, which has an upper limit—the total amount of gold atoms on Earth, or in the solar system if you're inclined to mine meteors. It's not called "Digital Gold" for nothing.

This kind of scarcity has its flip side. When assets reliably rise in value, they are great to own—and hard to let go of. So if your Bitcoin keeps appreciating, why would you spend it? If everyone is incentivized to hoard, how do you build an economy on that asset? This is a familiar problem, and one that gold has faced for centuries. It's excellent collateral, but a poor medium for everyday exchange.

One emerging answer, which excites me, is to treat Bitcoin the same way as gold. Instead of selling it, you lock up your BTC as collateral and borrow against it. You would normally do this in the form of stablecoins, namely digital tokens that are always worth a dollar. You get liquidity without any need to give up the asset you believe in. This is the logic behind systems being built to strengthen and expand the Bitcoin economy: hold scarce assets for the long term, use them productively as collateral, and let the economy operate on top.

WHY IS "SELF-CUSTODY" IMPORTANT?

In the finance you're probably familiar with (traditional finance), you own your money in perpetuity—until you don't. Your bank can intervene without even telling you. It can freeze your account, block your payments, confiscate your funds, or deny you access. During Argentina's 2001 financial crisis, millions of people had their accounts frozen. Those with US dollars lost more than half their deposit when they were forced to convert to pesos at punitive rates. In 2013, the Bank of Cyprus confiscated almost half of uninsured bank deposits over EUR100,000 as part of a bail-in. Russia's recent restrictions on cash withdrawals show how quickly access to funds can be limited when the country let banks block or limit ATM cash withdrawals. Transactions were flagged as suspicious even when they were a legitimate part of everyday operations. The result: One in three Russians had their transactions blocked.

Bitcoin provides the option of self-custody. If you hold your own private keys, you and only you control your coins. No bank or government can intervene.

And because Bitcoin isn't tied to any state or payment company, it also ignores borders. If you have an internet connection, you can send or receive Bitcoin (BTC). No gatekeepers. No permissions. It's a financial system built to be neutral, global, and unseizable—where ownership is enforced not by trust, but by code. You may have noticed that many people choose to place their Bitcoin with a third party, or custodian. While this might seem ironic, it does not undermine the core idea of Bitcoin. There's a difference between choosing to let someone else manage your Bitcoin and being required to do so.

To quote Satoshi from the white paper, Bitcoin is "an electronic payment system based on cryptographic proof instead of trust, allowing any two willing parties to transact *directly with each other* (my italics) without the need for a trusted third party."

CAN BITCOIN PAYMENTS BE REVERSED?

Bitcoin isn't just about sending money faster. It's about removing the layers of intermediaries that make traditional payments costly, reversible, and slow. In the fiat world—the old system of government-backed currencies—money hops between banks, gateways, and clearinghouses. It's a relay race. Bitcoin settles directly on the blockchain. Once a transaction is included in a block, each new block added on top is a *confirmation*. After approximately six confirmations (about an hour), the payment is economically final, meaning that reversing it would demand an extraordinarily costly chain re-organization. The electricity for the hash power would mean the reversal is not viable. In practice, there are no chargebacks or dispute forms because reversing a confirmed transaction is prohibitively expensive.

The Conceptual Leap to Ethereum

So far, we've talked about Bitcoin. But Bitcoin didn't just launch a currency—it launched a whole category of programmable blockchains. The principles we've explored so far—radical transparency, decentralization, self-custody, and finality—weren't confined to Bitcoin alone. They became the blueprint for a new wave of blockchains. Not all retained Bitcoin's hard cap, but most inherited the idea that trust could be replaced by software and incentives.

Arguably the most important new blockchain to date has been *Ethereum*. It was the brainchild of a teenager named Vitalik Buterin (universally known in the crypto community simply as "Vitalik"), whom I met shortly after the 2013 conference. He was lanky, fast-talking, and intensely focused—unlike any tech founder I'd met before.

He reached out to me while visiting Israel, after the conference, saying he wanted to talk, and hear more about the ZK cryptography I was working on. I often made time for smart young people, so we met for hummus at the Technion, where I was working at the time as a professor of theoretical computer science. He was writing about Bitcoin, but already had his eyes on a bigger idea—a "world computer." Just weeks after our meeting, he released a yellow paper outlining the concept.

Soon after publishing the Ethereum yellow paper, Vitalik contacted me again. He asked if I wanted to be involved, starting with reviewing the yellow paper. I said no. The project sounded brilliant—but also risky. At the time, crypto was a legal gray zone. I remember telling my wife, "Best case, he ends up in jail. Worst case, he ends up with a bullet in his head." I didn't want to be part of the core team. Later, and until this day, I lament that decision. If I ever get a time machine, I'll use it to go back in time and answer, "Yes!"

But I admired Ethereum. I believed in its potential. While I stayed away from its founding, my involvement would become central later—especially in helping it scale to support mass use. That's a story we'll return to soon.

Vitalik's Ethereum goes way beyond bypassing the bank. It's a shared online space with no owner and no limits, where anyone can upload and run software.

Where Bitcoin was designed for a single purpose—to let people send and store digital money without a central authority—Ethereum was designed as a general-purpose platform. It's a simple distinction. You can think of Bitcoin as a calculator: focused, reliable, unchangeable. By contrast, Ethereum aimed to be a full computer. The big innovation was the "smart contract"—small pieces of code that anyone could deploy, which would then run exactly as written, on a network no one controls. That made Ethereum programmable in a way Bitcoin was never meant to be.

To me, this is one of the most quietly revolutionary ideas we've come up with. But you'd never guess it from the way people usually describe it. They call Ethereum a "neutral settlement layer" or an "execution environment for smart contracts"—terms that sound like they belong in a white paper, not everyday life. What they really mean is this: We now have a shared system where anyone, anywhere, can make agreements that don't need an intermediary to enforce. No bank, no broker, no backroom. Just rules, written in code, that run automatically and can't be tampered with. That's power shifting hands.

A year after Ethereum went live, a different answer to Bitcoin's limits appeared. In 2016, Zcash sprung to life, focused not on programmability (making blockchain do more) but on privacy (making it do the same things as Bitcoin, but privately). Where Ethereum expanded what blockchains could do, Zcash pushed on what blockchains could hide. I was a co-founder of Zcash, and one of the architects of its privacy cryptography—a story we'll return to later in the book.

At this point I'll give you a small peek into where all of this is going. Another problem was emerging. As more people joined these networks, the systems struggled to keep up. Transactions slowed. Fees spiked. Suddenly the core promise—open access—was under threat.

In 2018, I co-founded StarkWare to help address that: not by changing the rules, but by scaling the systems. Armed with novel cryptography, we set out to help blockchains handle far more activity—without losing the decentralization and trust guarantees that made them worth caring about in the first place. And that, in turn, triggered the founding of Starknet, one of the most exciting blockchains in existence today—a general-purpose platform, which is the concept we discussed above in relation to Ethereum, but one that "anchors" to other blockchains to deliver mass scale.

Now that we have outlined the brave new worlds opened up by blockchain, it is time to bring in my co-author, Nathan. He didn't arrive in this world as a computer scientist. He arrived as a journalist, trained to distill complex ideas into a few hundred words. When he first encountered Ethereum, his reaction was that this is one of the most important stories in the world—but it's being told terribly. The ideas and ideals are remarkable, but outside the echo chamber of Ethereans, the narrative falls flat. That's exactly why I want to hand the pen to him here—to connect Ethereum's potential with the lives we actually live and to examine how the story has so often been told wrong.

CHAPTER 5

Beyond Currency: Blockchain as Infrastructure

Hi, I'm Nathan, and during 25-plus years in journalism, the stories that have gotten me most excited have always had the same ingredients. I am referring to the stories that left me sitting in my driveway for some extra research before joining the family or that made me wake up editors to tell them they've got something special. The stories were about out-of-the-box thinking, charismatic people, eccentricity, vision, and a moment in time when you can feel it all coming together. The Ethereum Community Conference (ETHCC) had all of this—in spades.

Join me in your mind's eye at this annual gathering of the global Ethereum community. It's probably the biggest of the many Ethereum conferences that take place each year. The vibe? Bizarre, energetic, and oddly exciting. The venue is usually a bit grungy. The Ethereum crowd doesn't have the same flashiness as Eli saw at the early Bitcoin conferences that featured cars and models. The air-conditioning and food can be unpredictable, but the WiFi is good and that's what matters. Ethereans want to be countercultural, even as they court mainstream adoption.

You'll see hoodies and branded swag, odd people in odd outfits—maybe unicorn-themed—and some who insist on being known only by their X handles. You're more likely to see someone present on stage from behind a mask (yes, that does happen) than attend in a suit (almost unseen). Some are here with close friends; others are meeting online collaborators face-to-face for the first time. I find it exhilarating—sometimes looking at the scene as an insider, part of it all, given that these days I work alongside Eli at StarkWare. And just as exhilarating when I shift perspective, put on my journalist glasses, and take it in from the outside, clocking the story as it unfolds.

Now, there are two things you should know about Ethereum conferences. First, everyone loves to talk. Second, they love to talk so much that hardly anyone actually attends the sessions. The panels and keynotes are relative sideshows. The real action happens in stairwells, corridors, and coffee lines. That's where people trade ideas, pitch projects, and find collaborators. There's a buzz—the thrill of being surrounded by people who don't just understand you; they speak your language.

And this is where the problem begins.

If you're an outsider trying to understand this world, it can be maddening. Show up and ask, "Why is Ethereum important?" and you'll find plenty of people eager to explain. But don't expect clarity. Expect a verbal waltz.

"It's decentralized," they'll say.

"Okay, but why does that matter?"

"Well, it's trustless."

"And why's that good?"

"Because it enables permissionless innovation."

"What kind of innovation?"

"Things like composability, censorship resistance, and decentralization!"

It spirals. You'll hear about block explorers for exploring blocks, decentralized exchanges for exchanging tokens, scaling layers for scaling, and a bunch of things that are likely to sound even more gobbledygook, like oracles for feeding in real-world data, gas fees, bridges, ZK-rollups.

And then, somewhere in your exasperation, you'll say, "Right. But what is this for? What's actually being built that helps people in their everyday lives? What's the thing I walk away with, besides understanding a new set of acronyms?"

The Ethereum Model
The story here is that the world has changed.

We're more global than ever in how we work and interact. But many of the old ways we used to establish trust—like knowing someone's family, reputation, or place in the village—don't travel with us online. And the fallback—relying on shared legal systems to enforce contracts—breaks down when we're spread across time zones and jurisdictions. Try chasing a few hundred dollars in small claims court across borders. Good luck.

Our shared space now is digital. But the way we make, manage, and enforce agreements is still based on tweaks to methods we've used for centuries: signatures, trust, and maybe a lawyer if things go sideways. Where we have tried to modernize things, we've done it by handing enormous power to single companies—platforms that act as both service provider and judge.

I once used an online platform to hire a freelancer. She did good work. Then, without warning, the platform banned her. The reason? She'd included her phone number on a CV—technically a violation of their terms. That was it. Her account was suspended, and she wasn't paid for the work she'd already done. The platform made the decision unilaterally. Their terms gave them that power. She had no appeal, no recourse, no voice.

This is how many of our systems operate now: opaque, centralized, and governed by private rulebooks inside walled gardens of big tech.

Ethereum offers a different model. It runs on programmable, immutable contracts—rules written in code, open to all, and visible upfront. They can't be rewritten quietly or enforced arbitrarily. That's the power of decentralization.

Anyone and everyone can understand why Ethereum matters. It matters because our day-to-day existence increasingly relies on us living in a space that isn't under my government's rule or yours—it's cyberspace. The pre-internet ways of governing our interactions often don't work in this new world. Here, we need new solutions.

If you take one thing from this chapter, remember this: You don't need to be a coding expert or a cryptocurrency investor to understand why it all matters—the point is simply that the world has changed.

Just as a handshake—and, in another era, a betrothal—no longer seals a business deal, the protocols of a few decades ago are already outdated.

Private businesses offer some solutions to the newfound needs of online life. But that's like handing over the policing of streets to a private security company that has the right to banish you—or to insist that you hop instead of walk—without accountability. Our public space needs to run smoothly and with accountability. That's the vision of Ethereum and other general-purpose blockchains that have followed in its footsteps.

By *general-purpose*, I mean blockchains not built for one narrow task (like only moving money) but for hosting open-ended software: programs, agreements, organizations, and tools that anyone can deploy and no one can unilaterally shut down.

The Fragility of Records

Money gets most of the attention when people talk about blockchain. But money is only one kind of record. And in everyday life, many of the records that matter most to us aren't financial at all.

Take a moment to think about the documents that are important to you. Property deeds. Birth certificates. Marriage licenses. Academic records. Medical histories. Contracts. Wills.

These are records meant to last decades—sometimes lifetimes, and beyond. They can determine where you're allowed to live, who you are in the eyes of the law, what rights you have, and what you can pass on to your children.

And yet we often forget how fragile these records really are. Who holds the five most important documents in your life? Where do they get their stamp of legitimacy? Who keeps the authoritative copy?

Or take something more common. If you have a dispute with your employer about the terms of your contract, what happens? Each of you digs out the copy you signed, checks if you're on the same page, and then argues the point. And if you've lost your copy—as many have—you're left relying on the employer's version. No choice. But should that really be how it works? Shouldn't there be a neutrally held, authoritative copy of such important documents?

I have a relative who lived in a house she had inherited. When she came to move homes, selling it should have been simple. But it became a bureaucratic maze for one reason: the original deeds couldn't be found. Government offices didn't have them. Lawyers had discarded old files. Wrong of them, certainly—but what were you going to do about it?

Archives yielded nothing. Everyone involved was trying their best—and still, no one could say with certainty where the true record lived. We use the idiom "safe as houses," yet ironically, this sturdy structure of bricks and mortar couldn't yield its liquidity, because proof of ownership had vanished.

This is just one of millions of examples of how we need better, more robust ways of storing our documents. Ways that aren't dependent on single links to keep everything running. Even today, in an advanced country like the United States, when someone dies the inheritance process depends on family knowing to go to the right lawyer with the right document in his or her safe. And if another lawyer or family member claims to have a different authoritative copy? Or a million other curveballs? It's no surprise that many family arguments are started over inheritance.

There are so many hidden weaknesses in our document systems. They rely on continuity—on offices staying open, databases being maintained, files not being lost, corrupted, deleted, or quietly deprioritized. Even when no one is malicious, records fail simply because time passes, systems change, and responsibility diffuses.

People mistakenly believe that the problem, and the fix, is technology. Build the right technology systems to store everything. But technology is only part of the puzzle. Consensus is the other piece. In fact, the more technologically advanced we become, the greater the need for consensus—as anyone can produce what look like official documents in minutes using AI. What we need are ways to prove beyond doubt which documents are legitimate, authoritative copies.

Blockchains outperform traditional databases precisely where continuity matters most.

Who runs traditional databases? A single body. They can edit it, migrate it, decommission it, or shut it down. What about a blockchain? As we have discussed, it's a shared public record that doesn't belong to any one organization. The moment that information is written to it, it doesn't depend on a single office, server, or authority continuing to exist. The record survives because it's copied, verified, and preserved collectively.

This has the potential to change something fundamental for the documents that matter. Instead of expecting institutions to safeguard our records indefinitely, we can anchor them in a system designed to remember.

And before we have visions of our birth certificates being on display for all to see our age, this doesn't mean putting sensitive documents on public display. It means anchoring proof—timestamps, hashes, ownership claims, attestations—so that the existence and integrity of a document can always be verified, even decades later. You don't have to trust that someone else kept the file. You can prove that it existed, that it hasn't been altered, and that it's connected to you.

Money, documents, identity, and rules are in truth all parts of public record keeping.

Money is really a record of who owes what to whom. Identity is a record: who you are, what credentials you hold, what claims you can make. Contracts are records of agreements. Governance is a record of decisions and rules. When these records are fragmented across banks, registries, corporations, and governments, power concentrates in the hands of whoever controls the database.

What societies need is a sturdy foundation, on which everyone agrees, that can support all of this. Blockchain can deliver a shared layer of integrity beneath all of this—a system where records live independently of any one institution. It's a realm where individuals can selectively prove facts about themselves without surrendering full control of their data.

When I write of how I foresee blockchain becoming a norm, I see it as a unified infrastructure for money, documents, identity, rules, and coordination, built around durability rather than discretion. Not a replacement for institutions, but a backstop against their failure. I see it as a system designed for the long arc of human life, not the lifespan of a database. And to use the word that I love, I see it as delivering integrity, and moving us to a digital life anchored in technology—Eli's shorthand, as I've said, is the Integrity Web—that serves us as a human race.

Some things are simply too important to be held by any single centralized body. When records matter for generations, memory itself has to be decentralized.

And not just for you and me. Whole societies depend on it.

We put enormous effort into requiring official records, transcripts, and archives—but then store them in formats that are fragile, centralized, and vulnerable. We should learn from this history. When record-keeping exists to preserve accountability, it only makes sense to store those records in a way no single actor can later erase or alter. Blockchain gives us that possibility. Not a perfect one, but a sturdier, fairer starting point.

During the mid-twentieth century, as the British Empire unwound, the Colonial Office launched a covert campaign known as Operation Legacy. As dozens of nations across Africa, Asia, and the Caribbean moved toward independence, British officials systematically destroyed or removed thousands of documents—files that could implicate the empire in abuse, exploitation, or misconduct. Some were burned. Others dumped at sea. Still others secretly shipped back to London, where they were hidden for decades.

This wasn't a failure of technology. The records existed. It was a failure of control. Of accountability. Of memory.

The Automated Contract

It gets even better. Blockchain doesn't just store records—it can animate them. A document on the blockchain need not be static. It can act.

Consider a contract. Not just as a piece of paper or a PDF, but as a live agreement that can execute itself. Triggered precisely when its terms are met, without needing a third party to interpret, enforce, or delay.

This brings us to a new kind of record: the automated contract. Let's explore.

Imagine you're an engineer, working in Dubai and sending home part of each monthly paycheck to your parents. Today, you rely on a remittance company that takes a cut (typically 1% to 3.5%), that insists you line up at a branch, and that can hold on to your funds for days before transferring them. You're signing up to a deal that spans time zones, legal systems, and cultures with a collaborator you barely know. You're at the mercy of their rules, their terms, and their conditions. And there are hidden costs, such as exchange rate margins that reduce the funds your parents actually receive.

A better option for you to get funds to your parents can be found with an *automated contract* (often called a *smart contract*), a code that runs on a general-purpose blockchain such as Ethereum. Instead of relying on a company or court, the code enforces the terms automatically when its conditions are met.

If you go down the route of blockchain-based smart contracts, you encounter a very different reality from that of remittance companies. When your salary arrives, the smart contract kicks into action. It automatically sends your parents the right amount. It converts your dirhams into digital tokens at the best available exchange rate.

Should you get a new job and want to alter the monthly amount, you just update a single field in the contract. The moment you stop working abroad, you revoke the contract—nothing gets frozen in legal limbo.

The smart contract isn't just digital convenience; it's digital stability. You upload the terms to a blockchain.

Let's take an example from a world I love: the world of podcasting. It's a space full of creative partnerships, recurring revenue, and all the usual frictions around fairness and follow-through. Suppose you're the host of a podcast, and your collaborator is the producer. Each time a new episode earns revenue, a smart contract on Ethereum automatically divides the payment, sending 50% to your wallet and 50% to your collaborator's. No lawyers, no follow-up emails. You don't even have to talk. Should there be a falling out, with bad blood between you and your co-creator, there are no awkward negotiations over your shared asset, because the rules you need are already baked in.

That's what immutability means. Neither of you can secretly change the contract once it's made. One person can't rewrite the terms, kick the other out, or take more than they're entitled to.

A natural question arises: if this is just software, couldn't someone edit it later? The answer is no—at least not on their own. The contract can only change in the specific ways it was designed to change. If an update requires both parties to agree, then both must approve it. If it doesn't, nothing happens.

Trust or good intentions don't underpin this system. It simply removes the option to cheat.

The beauty of smart contracts is that they can govern almost anything, not just money. For instance, journalists have already started timestamping their scoops on Ethereum so the public can be certain nothing was edited after publication.

Think about democracy. Say a board of directors is voting on whether a contentious company document should be made public. A blockchain like Ethereum can be used to conduct a secure and transparent vote. If the agreed majority—say three-quarters—vote in favor, the contract executes the agreed action—issuing a license, registering a claim, or triggering a payout. If not, nothing happens. The vote count can't be manipulated; nobody can intervene to release the document or to prevent its release. The blockchain is decentralized, which nobody can meddle with.

A corporate vote may not be the most exciting of uses or one that you really care about at all. Maybe corporate procedures aren't your thing, but if you've ever chased down the "final" version of a contract, you'll readily see the appeal of an automated system, one that nobody can screw up and one that can be used for any digital activity. No lawyers are needed to enforce agreements or argue about them; it's all hardwired into the execution instructions for the contract. Rules are visible to all and enforced by the network as a whole.

In short, blockchain has upped the game from money-only to money-plus-plus. UN aid agencies use it for refugee food vouchers, global shippers track freight documents on the blockchain, and even artists lock royalty splits into non-fungible token (NFT) contracts.

This evolution has spawned huge communities of enthusiasts who believe that soon enough all our important digital functions—from social media to gaming—will happen "on chain" and that every step in this direction will make the world a better place.

Why Adoption Happens: The Psychology of Control

The most powerful endorsement of blockchain might come not from technical users or ideological evangelists, but from people who are simply trying to live their lives with a little more certainty.

I had this in mind when I interviewed Bernardo Magri, a cryptographer and lecturer at the University of Manchester and the co-founder of the crypto investment firm Hashdex. Originally from Brazil, Magri has spent years researching the foundations of blockchain. Toward the end of our conversation, I asked where he thought the biggest uptake would come from. His answer caught me.

He said that mass adoption will only happen when the traditional financial system is "crumbling"—not in a collapse-the-world sense, but in something quieter and more localized. He described the feeling in places where inflation is volatile, where political interference is real, and where governments limit how and when people can move money. "People start feeling that they don't have control of anything," he said. "They don't actually own anything that they have."[1]

For Magri, the turn to blockchain isn't just practical; it's psychological. Blockchain enables people to regain some sense of control. "It's a way to escape inflation . . . to have some kind of custody . . . to have more guarantees that you can access your money." Or to put it another way, the shift is less about maximizing gains than about minimizing vulnerability.

Magri pointed to Argentina and Venezuela, where banknotes became so worthless that people burned them for heat. "Everybody is afraid," he said of his extended family still in Brazil. "They're unsure of what is going to happen. And I've seen more and more people asking and getting interested in cryptocurrencies because of that."

Beyond the technical tools and economic arguments lies something more universal: a psychological response to chaos. A human needs to feel anchored when the familiar markers—currency, contracts, rules—begin to blur.

This turn toward crypto doesn't require a systemic collapse. It doesn't take a hyperinflationary spiral or a sweeping dictatorship. Often the trigger is smaller: a freeze on international transfers, an unexplained delay at the bank, an article about new capital controls. The threshold doesn't need to be a catastrophe. Doubt will suffice. And once that doubt sets in, the appeal of something decentralized, borderless, and self-custodial becomes clear. It means money that isn't controlled by a single authority can move across borders as easily as an email, and stays in your hands—not locked behind a bank's permission slip.

As Magri puts it: "People don't want to feel at the mercy of systems they can't see or influence. They want to feel like they have a way out."

Wences Casares, an Argentine entrepreneur who later founded Xapo Bank, lived that reality. He grew up in Patagonia, where his family's savings were repeatedly destroyed by inflation and banking crises. For him, Bitcoin wasn't a speculative bet. It was a lifeline—a way to hold value and transact without fear of seizure or censorship.

In a 2018 interview with the *Unchained* podcast, Casares said, "I find that it's very hard to explain Bitcoin in the U.S. . . . Argentina is maybe one of the easiest. The U.S. maybe one of the hardest and I think it makes sense because when you talk about money to an American, it is a little bit like talking about water to a fish, you know; I'm sure that the fish doesn't even know that water exists. It is invisible to them. They won't know what you're talking about. Money has always worked for Americans. It has worked for them and for their parents and their grandparents."

"They always use the same form of money. In Argentina, each generation has discarded some form of currency, at least once, probably more than once. Imagine that for some crisis you could get rid of the dollar and you have a new currency. A new American currency that's called something different but not dollars. It sort of just changes significantly how you see money. You don't take it as this given instrument that works. But it makes you question a lot."[2]

Perspectives of those like Magri and Casares, who have seen the need first-hand, point to the deeper heart of crypto: not riches or contracts, but autonomy. The right to hold and use your own money, on your own terms—without intermediaries deciding when or whether you can.

CHAPTER 6

Social Media, AI, and the Gig Economy

This is Nathan here for another chapter before we hand it back to Eli, and I'm ready to take you on a journalist-style adventure to Scotland.

One of the most significant news stories of the past two to three decades is the way the internet has revolutionized our interactions with one another. It is a double-edged sword. We cannot imagine how much more severe the loneliness of the pandemic would have been were it not for social media; yet at the same time, there is cause for concern.

Let me paint you a picture. It's your birthday. Dozens of friends have shown up at your favorite bar, and you're excited to catch up and tell everyone your news. But when you get to the venue, they tell you there's one unbreakable rule.

They sit you down at the end of a long table, with your guests dotted around the room—some at high tops, some near the bar, some by the window. The rule is that you are not permitted to talk directly to your guests. Instead, you've been assigned a friendly waiter, who conveys the stories you want to tell them. He shares the anecdotes you want to share and passes around the photos you want to show.

The waiter hands you a cocktail, a gift from your friend in the far corner. The waiter then smiles and delivers a message from the friend: "How would you like to get the conversation with your friends started?" he asks politely.

You crack a joke. The waiter laughs, then dutifully runs off to all corners of the room to repeat it.

Birthdays are also a time for reflection, so next up, you share something more meaningful—your relief after a recent medical scare, with some graphic details. The waiter hesitates. "Hmm," he says, glancing toward the manager. "Might kill the mood. We'll send that to just a few people in the back."

Next, you share a story about your tour of a vineyard in Bordeaux. The waiter is smiling again. "Well, that's going to prompt a rush on the bar for wine orders. Let's tell everyone."

Then you turn to politics. Your opinion is nuanced and takes a couple of minutes to explain. The waiter looks at his watch and yawns. Nuanced but controversial. Your conclusion won't please everyone. The waiter stiffens. "That one's tricky. Dull and controversial. Might bore some guests and upset others. They may leave, and that will hit drink sales. I'll skip it."

You have a selection of photos on your phone: your grandmother in the hospital, with breathing tubes and a 90th birthday balloon. Your son at a war memorial during a recent school trip. A family trip to Disneyland. The waiter flips through them like a sommelier checking corks. "The grandma one is a mood killer; the war memorial one is too somber. I'll just show them to your boring work friends. But the Disneyland pics I'll show to everyone, especially as this venue has a promo for the upcoming Disney movie."

Absurd, right?

And yet this is an approximation of how social media works today.

Sure, we can still have one-on-one chats—digital coffee dates via text or direct messages (DMs). But when we try to speak to groups, to host the virtual equivalent of a gathering—a party, a reunion, a shared experience—we're no longer talking to our friends. We're talking to the waiter, or, more accurately, the *algorithm*.

The platform decides who hears what. Which story spreads? Which photo gets seen? Which ideas make the rounds and which die quietly in the corner, ignored not because they lacked relevance, but because they weren't good for business?

This isn't tinfoil-hat stuff. It's not about secret agendas. It's about incentives. Social media companies are in the business of maximizing engagement (and revenue). And the way they do that is dictated by the algorithm.

I was thinking about all this while sitting in an office at the University of Edinburgh, speaking with Professor Aggelos Kiayias.[1]

Outside, the city was buzzing with crowds who descend on the town every August for "The Fringe," the world's largest performing arts festival.

Inside, at the School of Informatics, a bastion of research in computing science, artificial intelligence, and blockchain, I asked Kiayias what he sees as the biggest problem in the digital space.

He said that everything we do online—our digital speech, our connections, our very ability to converse—is mediated by platforms we neither control nor fully understand. This, he said, is the real problem. Not just privacy. Not just data. But power—who holds it and who gets sidelined.

The conversation that followed wasn't a diatribe against tech companies. Instead, Kiayias lingered on the problem itself: every word we type, every photo we share, is filtered through corporate platforms whose algorithms silently decide what rises—and what sinks.

Until we realize how strange that arrangement is, passing each meaningful moment through a waiter with their own incentives, we can't quite appreciate why Kiayias believes we need a new model.

What makes the current social media setup so unsettling is not just the fact that someone else controls the conversation. It's also that there is no obvious way to challenge it. The waiter's decision is final and if he decides your story isn't worth repeating, you are not entitled to any explanation. You aren't exactly being censored but something essential has been taken from you: agency. The uncertainty and the quiet sense of powerlessness are features, rather than bugs, of a system that is always stacked to favor tech giants. Mediation is invisible, accountability is absent, and responsibility is always somewhere else.

Scotland feels like an apt place to think about these questions, and not just because I took full advantage of the local whisky distilleries, which put me in a very pondering mood. Scotland has a long history of grappling with how complex systems function without central command. Back in the 18th century, philosophers like Adam Smith, often remembered as the "markets guy," and David Hume asked deep questions about how order, trust, and cooperation emerge when no single authority is in charge.

They expended much brainpower on how shared rules and incentives coordinate behavior at scale. As I walked into the University of Edinburgh to talk blockchain, it struck me that we're still wrestling with the same problem today. Today, the systems run faster, reach further, and hide their rules more carefully. Before turning to what might replace them, it's worth looking more closely at how these systems actually work—and where they fail.

The Algorithm

Many people are surprised by the fact that when you post a photo, a memory, an article, or a personal reflection on social media, it doesn't automatically appear in your friends' feeds. It's not like a message sliding into a mailbox. Even if they scroll for hours, they may not see your post. Why? Because there is third-party intervention.

You hand your message to the birthday party "waiter"—in this case, an invisible, automated sorting mechanism called an *algorithm*. The algorithm determines how many people will view it, who specifically, when, and in what context—if at all.

What is an algorithm? It's a set of rules or instructions compiled to solve a problem or make a decision. In the social media context, algorithms rank and filter content. They are the decision-makers deep in the social media platform's coding that determine which posts float to the top of someone's feed, which disappear into the void, and which go viral. The platforms—Facebook, Instagram, TikTok, YouTube, X (formerly Twitter)—each have their own proprietary algorithms, but the logic is similar: maximize engagement.

And that's where things get complicated.

Engagement refers to the number of clicks, likes, shares, and comments a piece of content receives. Algorithms are trained to identify content that is more likely to generate interaction and then promote that content. It doesn't matter whether users want to interact with it because it's accurate, enlightening, meaningful, or absurd. What matters is that it performs well.

Back in 2025, for several weeks, everyone was talking about a "kiss cam scandal." A married CEO was caught on camera with a colleague at a Coldplay concert. Andy Byron and his data startup Astronomer were hardly household names. But the algorithms of every social media platform had a field day with this story, pushing it and all the memes and comments that followed, far and wide—not because it was important, but because it got high engagement.

The algorithm doesn't care whether the emotion is positive or negative. It cares only that you don't look away.

So why does engagement matter so much? Because social media companies make their money—nearly all of it—through advertising. It's their lifeblood. The more time users spend on the platform, the more ads they will be shown. The more interaction there is, the more data they gather about their audience. The more precise the data, the higher the value of the advertising space.

Ads mean revenue. In traditional media, such as magazines and newspapers, it's the professionally-produced content, paid for by the publisher, that attracts readers. Advertisers pay to reach those readers. In social media, it's the freely-produced content—your photographs, your videos, your memories, your opinions—that attracts viewers and drives advertising revenue. So Facebook, YouTube, Instagram, and the other platforms need you, the viewer, to keep posting your free content. And at the same time, they need you, the viewer, to keep viewing other people's content. More engagement means more ads are seen, and more ads being seen means more money is made.

In the early days, social media was a digital town square—a place to swap recipes and post cute cat videos. Today, Facebook influences elections, TikTok dictates music trends, and YouTube rewires education. They all radicalize a generation hooked on screens.

Why Worry?

The concern is that opaque, engagement-maximizing algorithms on social platforms decide who sees what and how far it spreads because that power is largely unregulated. Most countries have a watchdog to oversee traditional media, but social media platforms, with their immense power, have minimal accountability. If a public broadcaster distorts the news, a regulator will typically intervene. If a local council mismanages resources, there's an election. If a shop mistreats a customer, consumer protection laws apply. But social media is the Wild West.

The algorithms that make decisions about what happens to your posts are invariably black boxes—you can see what goes in and what comes out, but even the experts have no idea what happens inside.

The platforms operate without a vote and a constitution, and they can shut down your account at will. Most have an internal appeals process, but it is opaque, to say the least.

In other spheres of life, we have mechanisms for recourse. But with social media we do not. If we had reliable ways to oversee or influence how the platforms operate, we might not need to be so worried.

Unfortunately, with social media, there is hardly any accountability over which issues rise and which are ignored, which views dominate and which are pushed to the sidelines, which conversations take hold and which aren't deemed worthy of exposure. The hood of an algorithm can't be cracked open for us to take a peek. We can't meaningfully challenge its decisions. Even the laws that exist—regarding data privacy, competition, or content moderation—were not designed to address the sheer scale, speed, and subtlety of these digital infrastructures.

I'm not out to vilify social media companies. They are not villains, but rather businesses that are playing the system. They are operating beyond the scope of outdated frameworks that are supposed to safeguard fairness and accountability in public life. The platforms haven't hijacked society. What they have done is to move faster and smarter than the structures meant to guide and regulate them. The result is that we live inside information systems that are extraordinarily powerful—but almost entirely unaccountable.

These systems neither love us (though they are programmed to make us feel like they do) nor hate us. In reality, they just care about what can be measured, because that's what generates money for them. And what can be measured, above all, is what gets clicked.

How Can Blockchain Help?

So what does blockchain actually offer in this context? How would social media apps work differently if they were built on blockchain or found ways of using blockchain to regulate their operation?

First, blockchain offers *permanence* and *accountability*. Once information is added to a blockchain, it is effectively permanent, tamper-evident, and append-only. Changes, if they happen at all, require broad public coordination and leave a visible trail—no quiet alteration or erasure. That doesn't mean every social media post needs to be locked in forever, but it does mean key decisions, like why a post was taken down or who made that call, can be recorded in a way that can't be edited in secret later. That creates a basic level of auditability: not absolute transparency or immutability, but a nearly immutable record that's enough to check whether policies are being applied fairly—or inconsistently.

The stakes are far from hypothetical. A company or nonprofit that's spent many years and many hundreds of thousands of dollars building up a digital presence—followers, brand recognition, and customer trust—can have its account flagged by an algorithm for violating a policy. There's no warning, no dialogue, no appeal. The account is removed, and the carefully cultivated audience is gone. This happens more often than most people realize, and it happens inside opaque systems where even the people in charge are often unable to fully explain a specific decision.

Because there's no visibility regarding how decisions are made, those affected have no redress. Blockchain can't prevent mistakes from happening, but it can ensure there's a record—and that record can be used to ask fundamental questions, demand honest answers, and appeal decisions in a structured way.

Second, blockchain offers *transparent decision-making*. Blockchain lets us build systems where the rules that shape what we see—what gets ranked, promoted, or blocked—aren't hidden behind closed doors. They can be made public in a way that's both understandable and verifiable. Blockchains can add cryptographic guarantees that the published rules were the ones applied, effectively ensuring that outsiders can verify behavior without having to trust the operator. This doesn't mean there has to be one global standard. But it does mean we could have a real choice: different content-sorting methods for various needs, each one clearly defined and open to scrutiny. If a platform promises to treat your post in a certain way, you'd be able to check whether it does.

Third, blockchain offers *identity verification*. People are able to prove specific aspects of their identity—without revealing everything.

A journalist could sign an article to confirm it's really theirs. A fact-checker could prove they're authorized to issue a correction. This doesn't require them to expose their whole identity, but it does allow trust to form where it matters—without defaulting to either total exposure or complete anonymity.

Fourth, blockchain enables *clear processes for appeals*. Today, if your content is removed or your account is disabled, your options are minimal. You click a "dispute" button and wait, often with no response. A blockchain-based system could make that process far more structured. Disputes could be logged, timelines tracked, and decisions reviewed—not just by internal moderators, but through open, rule-based mechanisms, such as a small-claims court for digital rights.

Fifth, blockchain offers *system-level rights that can't be quietly rewritten*. On most platforms today, your rights are set by terms of service, which can be changed at any time. With blockchain, it's possible to define specific user rights as part of the system itself, such as the right to access your data, the right to know how your content is ranked, or the right to move your content elsewhere. These aren't features. They're guarantees, locked into the infrastructure.

Finally, and perhaps most importantly, comes one of Eli's favorite phrases: Blockchain enables you to *own your life*. It's easy to think the problem of online control has already been solved. "But I have privacy settings," people say. "I can choose who sees my posts." And it's true—to a point. Today's platforms let you toggle visibility, limit sharing, and even delete your content. But the system in which all of that happens is entirely beyond your control. The platform still stores your data. It still controls the distribution. It still decides, through its algorithms, who actually sees what, when, and under what conditions. And it can change those terms tomorrow, without asking.

This is the deeper truth: In the current model, you're not just posting on a platform—you're freely handing over your digital life. Your photos, your thoughts, your creative work, your social history—they live on someone else's servers, under someone else's rules. The platform doesn't just host your content; it dictates how your digital self appears and exploits what it learns about you to try to sell you stuff.

Blockchain offers a different path in the world of social media and indeed the broader internet—one where you can take part without surrendering control. With blockchain-based systems, you are in direct control of your identity, your content, and your connections. You can prove authorship, carry your data across platforms, and set rules that are enforced automatically.

You become the custodian of your digital life—not just a guest on someone else's platform. You don't have to rely on promises that your data won't be misused. The system is built so that misuse isn't a matter of trust; it's a matter of technical impossibility, or at least full transparency. You decide what to share, with whom, and for how long. If a platform wants to access your data—to personalize content or serve ads—it has to request it, and you have the power to approve, limit, or deny that request entirely. The architecture respects your agency. You don't just use the internet. You own your corner of it.

A thousand years ago, most people worked the land, yet the number who owned it was relatively small. In many places, peasants tilled fields, while ownership and profit flowed upward to a small number of noblemen. Today, in the digital sphere, the pattern is familiar. We all labor on digital land. We post our experiences, create, connect—but control and value accrue to a handful of platforms. Our own life experiences become monetized by the digital giants. Blockchain represents a structural break from that model. For the first time, ownership can sit with the participant rather than the landlord. This is what I mean when I say: you own your life.

Blockchain will become increasingly relevant in the realm of social media. It's true that there have already been attempts in this direction, and none has yet achieved major success. But that says less about the underlying advantages for users, and more about the massive marketing budgets, refined user interfaces, and sheer critical mass enjoyed by the world's biggest platforms. Usage patterns, however, are not fixed. They evolve.

Artificial Intelligence

I asked Professor Kiayias whether the kind of accountability he envisions for social media could also be applied to artificial intelligence? With AI systems now deeply embedded in daily life, it felt like a very relevant question to ask. After all, much like the platforms that deliver our social feeds, AI systems often work in ways that are entirely hidden from the people they affect.

Kiayias didn't hesitate. "The same accountability principles must apply to AI," he said.

An emerging problem extends across every domain touched by AI, he said. It is the lack of transparency in decision-making. Hiring systems use AI models to screen job applications, for example. A candidate rarely has any idea why they were rejected. Was it their qualifications, a keyword match, or a bias buried deep in the training data? Might it even be that the model has been, outrageously, trained to downgrade applications from women of a childbearing age to avoid taking candidates who may go on maternity leave? There's no way of knowing, no record to inspect, no consistent way to appeal.

What blockchain offers, he said, is a way to start addressing the transparency and accountability problem—not by changing how models think, but by changing how their decisions are recorded and reviewed.

Blockchain systems can verify that something happened the right way without exposing all the raw details. In fact, this is precisely Eli's area of expertise: so-called zero-knowledge technology, which has been mentioned earlier in the book and will be discussed in more depth later. Instead of revealing every input, zero-knowledge blockchain systems produce a cryptographic proof that the rules were followed and that the outcome is correct. Often that outcome is a simple bottom line—who is recorded as owning which funds—but the idea extends far beyond money, and turns out to be a good fit for certain aspects of AI.

Let's take a really concrete example. If you apply for a job, there's a high chance your application is first scanned by an AI system—and only top-ranked ones reach human eyes. But what values is that AI built on? Does it carry biases against women, certain ethnic groups, or people from specific regions? Is it aligned with the company's stated equal-opportunity policies?

As a 2025 study observed:

> Artificial Intelligence (AI) has transformed Human Resource Management (HRM), offering efficiency and objectivity in processes like recruitment and performance evaluation. However, AI-driven HRM systems are not without challenges, particularly regarding the biases embedded in their design,

which can disproportionately affect marginalized groups—including non-binary individuals, women, racial minorities, and persons with disabilities.[2]

On something this important, there should be a compliance stamp—a mark showing that the code matches the stated principles, and that it hasn't been quietly changed. This is precisely the type of accountability that zero-knowledge-enabled blockchains can deliver.

How do the HR department and the CEO check those values? They don't need to see every internal signal or line of code. They need assurance that the system prioritizes professional experience and other relevant factors—and proof that it does so consistently.

In such an instance, and others in which blockchain can be used to deliver accountability to uses of AI, companies would not need to expose every internal parameter of their models, but the technology would be used to create a verifiable trail. The audit log could record when a model was updated, what kind of change was made, and whether that update affected how it responded to certain types of input.

Kiayias also spoke about where training data comes from. Today, most large-scale AI models are trained on vast collections of data automatically collected from the internet—which is a problem. The AI is a hungry beast that must be fed constantly, so its diet can be a matter of quantity over quality. Oversight over the sources, and clarity of what they are, can be limited. Kiayias suggests blockchain could help here, by tracking the provenance of that data: who contributed it, under what terms, and whether consent was obtained. In domains that are sensitive and where AI information can literally be matters of life and death, such as healthcare or law, that kind of traceability isn't just useful—it's essential.

And if a model starts misbehaving—making unfair recommendations, giving harmful advice, or reflecting bias—blockchain-based systems could help structure the process of challenge and appeal. Not just the vague hope of "submit feedback," but a real record that can be reviewed and challenged in a system that can be held to account.

What about large language models (LLMs) like ChatGPT? Can they be "bought"? If I ask about climate change, will I get the same answer wherever in the world I'm located? Or might answers diverge, not due to language or nuance, but because one region has a commercial agreement in place? For example, a sponsorship deal could nudge answers to favor a product, or a government directive in a given country could suppress certain responses.

The idea of private company interference via large language models like ChatGPT or Google's Gemini isn't far-fetched, but it's structurally possible and easy for coders to achieve since private companies maintain LLMs. Most are under no binding obligation to disclose how or why behavior might change. In theory, a language model could sign a sponsorship deal with a soft drinks company and begin suggesting, however indirectly, that brushing teeth with cola is medically sound. It's crazy—but totally possible. In fact, we already see softer versions of this today in AI systems that are often tuned to reflect the values and commercial priorities of their parent companies. Whether it's X's Grok or Google's Gemini, the answers they produce are shaped, subtly or not, by corporate context. Kiayias argues that even if we can't prevent such distortions, we should at least be able to know that they are happening in order to make informed decisions about, for example, which AI tool to use and which to avoid.

That's where blockchain offers a vital solution.

Kiayias emphasized that introducing checks and balances doesn't mean putting the entire model on a blockchain. That would be unwieldy and, in many cases, technically impossible. Instead, it's about recording just enough of the system's logic and evolution to create accountability: when decisions were made, by whom, under what rules, and whether there's a pathway for contesting them.

The goal isn't perfect AI. The aim is visible failures and answerable power. And in a world where more and more decisions are being made by code—determined automatically by computer programs, algorithms, or AI rather than humans—that visibility may be the difference between being governed by machines and coexisting with them under shared norms.

The Gig Economy

Let me shift now from a topic that's all about how we interact to one that's about how we work—or rather, how a growing segment of the world's population works. I'm talking about the *gig economy*.

The setting for my journalistic digging shifts here too—from Edinburgh in festival season to Cannes, a few weeks after all the red-carpet glamour has died down. The film stars are gone, but a different kind of energy fills the air—geekier, more intense, but no less ambitious. It's the Ethereum Community Conference—EthCC for short—that I mentioned earlier. That's where I met up with Harish Devarajan, a sharp thinker with a particular gift for spotting where systems bend and where they break.[3]

Devarajan is based in Chicago and has spent his career at the intersection of markets, math, and technology, and one of his many passions is serving on StarkWare's board. Over coffee one day at the conference, we found ourselves discussing not tokens or tech stacks, but Uber—or more precisely, the kind of economic structures that shape life for tens of millions of people today and how those structures might be rebuilt.

The gig marketplaces that increasingly dominate employment rely on the hidden plumbing of traditional off-chain systems, notes Devarajan. He is convinced that entirely new gig marketplaces can live on the blockchain.

Superficially, the gig economy appears to be a modern marvel. Platforms like Uber, DoorDash, and Grubhub offer flexibility, convenience, and rapid access to revenue. They provide work to millions. But they have also ushered in something of a dystopian reality, of people whose boss is an algorithm.

Algorithms determine which driver gets which job, how much they're paid, and how their performance is rated. All of this happens behind a digital curtain that is opaque, unaccountable, and nearly impossible to contest. The system appears to benefit the driver, but it functions as extractive: efficient in execution, but skewed in power to a boss whom workers never meet.

Devarajan says a much better version would not only be built on blockchain, but would actually embody blockchain values. Instead of a centralized company writing the rules and pocketing the profits, a digital cooperative of drivers could commission and govern the system themselves. Smart contracts—self-executing code stored on-chain—would handle all the logistics.

Blockchain could take care of ride matching, route optimization, and dynamic pricing. These contracts would be open-source and auditable, so every driver could see precisely how decisions were made. And drivers would be connected to one another, partners in the venture, possibly with a social element wrapped into the whole arrangement.

When a passenger pays their fare, the money does not go to a third party; funds move to the driver, minus only minimal network fees. Governance, too, would be decentralized: this would mean any change to the platform's rules would require a member's vote and would be implemented automatically if they approved. Drivers' reputation data, built up over years in some cases, would follow them if they switched from DoorDash to Grubhub. Today, it would simply be lost.

The technical stack—the combination of hardware and software—would be different, but so would the political economy; workers would be platform participants, not just data points in someone else's optimization function.

This kind of idea is not pie in the sky. In India, some gig platforms have already begun experimenting with new models—faster settlement and more equitable commissions—not because of ideology, but because infrastructure has made it possible. As Devarajan put it, this is about "civic recomposition." The internet, long dominated by rent-extracting platforms—big players taking big cuts—is starting to make room for ecosystems in which it's the participants who shape the rules. Blockchain enables that shift. It turns "users" back into stakeholders and becomes an obvious and better choice. For workers, it offers a pathway not just to earn, but to govern.

Blockchain as the Enabler

If the changes discussed in this chapter start to take hold, blockchain will emerge from its niche and become the infrastructure of economic participation. Systems that run our lives will exploit us less and be designed to reward us more—systems that manage income distribution, reputation, coordination, and rule-making.

In Devarajan's vision, blockchain platforms wouldn't compete by locking users in, but by empowering users outright. Immediate payment is just one of the benefits drivers would gain. They'd share in the protocols that built the platform, vote on commissions, and carry their work history to new networks. Immutable smart contracts and transparent audit logs would be there to mediate trust.

Redistributing value, agency, and trust should be at the crux of how we define human dignity and personal freedom. What starts as a technical architecture becomes a political architecture. And this is just the start—today's gig, content, or service economy becomes tomorrow's cooperative, network-owned ecosystem.

Throughout this chapter, and throughout my travels, the same core question emerges: Do we want platforms that serve us or systems that enable us? Blockchain can become the secure foundation of our digital lives. This discussion is not for utopia's sake, but for the sake of accountability, to liberate us and preserve our dignity.

CHAPTER 7

Roadblocks to Mass Adoption

In this very brief chapter, I'm picking the pen up again and shifting to the practical realities that stand in the way of building systems that live up to the ideals that my co-author Nathan just described. These ideals shape systems that scale, remain decentralized, and that don't force us to trade away the values that made blockchain worth caring about in the first place. We'll look at the real obstacles that have limited the widespread adoption of blockchain.

To begin, let's ask ourselves, If blockchain is so great, why isn't it everywhere already? Why are we reading about it rather than encountering it everywhere we go? If we can't clearly explain the obstacles to widespread use, we're probably spilling ink over a technology that isn't solving real problems.

Why exactly is blockchain so puny? Why can't it handle more transactions? Here's the thing: Blockchain design explicitly prioritizes security and minimizing reliance on any single party over raw throughput. This characteristic of blockchain isn't an accident or a fixable glitch. It's an unavoidable consequence of the all-are-invited ideal we discussed earlier in the book. It's an integral part of the design—a feature, not a bug.

This feature surprises people at first. But blockchain makes a deliberate trade-off: It chooses security and trust over speed by inviting everyone to operate it.

This limitation, scale, is just one of the three main roadblocks to mass adoption. Let's take a look at these structural factors that explain why blockchain has not, yet, become the norm.

Roadblock 1: Regulation

Rules are shifting and fragmented, meaning that the same token can be treated and regulated as a security (akin to stocks) in one place and a commodity (akin to corn and wheat) in another. Jurisdictions vary in terms of licensing for exchanges and stablecoins. Also slowing the adoption of blockchain are the added layers of compliance and paperwork that are required by the Know Your Customer (KYC) process, regulations against money laundering, and the so-called Travel Rule, which mandates that personal information must accompany certain digital asset transfers. Implementing the rules can be costly and time-consuming. In this context, small everyday purchases can create taxable events, making the use of cryptocurrency for day-to-day purposes cumbersome and challenging.

Roadblock 2: User Experience

Crypto has a usability problem—one so serious that many people are missing out on the most exciting apps: those truly anchored to the blockchain. The idea is compelling, but the tools are often clunky, the risks unclear, and the margin for error too high. As a result, most people experience crypto not through decentralized tools, but through custodial services—centralized platforms that feel more like banks than blockchains.

Earlier in the book, we talked about custody and self-custody: the difference between holding your own keys and trusting someone else to do it for you. What follows explains why, for many, self-custody remains out of reach—not due to lack of interest, but because the tools are still too hard to use.

The blockchain world can feel alien to newcomers—or worse, downright hostile. Just consider what users have to navigate:

In traditional crypto, you don't create an account with a username and password. You generate a seed phrase—a string of 12 or

24 random words—which becomes your only way to recover access. If you lose it, your assets are gone forever. There is no reset button. No customer support.

Instead of names or email addresses, you send money to long alphanumeric strings like 0x8f3Cf7ad23Cd3CaDbD9735AFf958023239c6A063. Mistype one character—yep, just a single one—and the funds are lost. Permanently.

Every action on the network costs a fee that is paid in cryptocurrency. Often known as "gas fees," these vary by time of day and network congestion—and they're rarely predictable. You can spend anywhere between fractions of a cent and $5 or more to send $10 (on the bright side, fees are usually independent of transaction size, so it'll cost the same fee to send $10 and $10,000,000).

Even after you pay, transactions can fail or hang without a clear reason. Sometimes you try to make a swap and it doesn't go through (no funds are taken but it's frustrating). Sometimes it takes 10 minutes, or longer. There's no help desk, and no, you can't switch the blockchain off and on again.

On-ramps—the systems that convert dollars or euros from your credit card or bank account into crypto—often feel more like wiring funds internationally than tapping to pay. They involve multiple steps, identity checks, delays. Even seasoned users find the process clunky.

And across the board, apps feel awkward. Signing up takes too long. Checking out is confusing. Interfaces vary wildly. Nothing feels smooth.

We're used to the frictionless ease of modern banking and shopping apps. By comparison, blockchain often feels like using the internet before browsers—powerful, but raw and unforgiving.

All of this is the "classic" crypto experience. And it is shifting. Each of these factors is changing—but not fast enough for the general public, en masse, to say "Yep, crypto is now intuitive."

Roadblock 3: The Scaling (or Tricky) Trilemma

If you try to solve blockchain's sluggishness, you will run headfirst into one of its core design challenges. Professionals who develop blockchain infrastructure and apps refer to this challenge as the *scaling trilemma*—a three-way dilemma that boils down to simultaneously upholding three competing values:

1. Decentralization (the everyone-is-invited ideal).
2. Security (resistance to attack or manipulation).
3. Scalability (the ability to serve millions—or billions—of users without breaking down).

All three sound essential—and they are. But here's the catch: In practice, you can usually only have two. One has to go.

Let's say you want *decentralization and security*. You've built a robust, trustless network—based on tech, not trust—where everyone helps verify transactions. But because everyone is involved, it's slow. That's the bottleneck you feel: not just in transaction speed, but in how well the system handles scale.

Want *security and scalability* (speed/throughput)? You'll need to streamline the decision-making process to keep things moving, often by appointing a central authority—just like banks or Visa. Fast, yes. But no longer decentralized, and as such you no longer truly own your life but are once again at the mercy of powerful centralized parties.

Want *decentralization and scalability*? That combination can work for low-stakes use cases—file sharing is the classic example. Protocols like BitTorrent show how millions of participants can coordinate and move data efficiently without a central authority. But if you are choosing the decentralization-scalability model for higher-stakes uses, you're probably cutting corners on security or spreading control too thin. The result: vulnerability to fraud or manipulation. You certainly would not route trillions of dollars through such a protocol; for that you would turn to Bitcoin.

In short, scalability isn't just speed. It's the ability to grow throughput without collapsing the other two competing values. When everyone gets a say, coordination takes time. That is the actual cost of decentralization.

And when the network, by design, works laboriously, it's all too easy to clog it. This is precisely why scaling isn't just a theoretical concern—it's urgent. A vivid example came in 2017 with CryptoKitties, a popular game on Ethereum which involved users "breeding" and trading digital cats.

Now, the point of an "on-chain" app is that it constantly "talks" to the blockchain, which means a large quantity of transactions happening. The game became so popular that it generated enough transactions to clog the entire network, slowing transactions and spiking fees. A single fun innovation nearly caused a meltdown, exposing how vulnerable blockchains were to congestion. It desperately highlighted the need for solutions that could scale with demand.

The scaling trilemma can feel like a dead end. The way through is a different approach, one that changes the trade-offs rather than picking one—and this will be the major focus in the chapters to come.

CHAPTER 8

The Magic of Proofs

In the last chapter, I discussed the roadblocks for scaling blockchains. Perhaps the oddest twist of my career is that I came to learn that, unknowingly, I had done the equivalent of inventing a method to clear roadblocks—before roads had ever been built.

Let me put it another way. Imagine you invented the perfect milk-frothing device—just before the world fell in love with cappuccinos. Or the ultimate material for screen protectors—right before smartphones hit the market. That's how my research on validity proofs felt when I walked into the 2013 Bitcoin conference. Work I'd pursued mostly for the intellectual thrill suddenly looked like the lever that could move blockchain's hardest problem: *scale*.

Let's take a moment to remind ourselves what we mean by a proof in math. It is a careful way of showing that something isn't just true in a few examples, but must be true in every case, even if the number of cases is infinite. It's how math replaces experiments and intuition commonly used in other branches of science with absolute certainty—which is precisely the quality of math that gets me excited.

I'd been working for years on an obscure branch of mathematics known as *validity proofs* or, more commonly, *zero-knowledge proofs*. But it was only when I walked into that conference that I realized what a critical role these proofs, whatever you call them, could play in blockchain scalability. Then and there it struck me that validity proofs could compress blockchain computation and scale them exponentially. As far as I knew I was the first person to see this and felt compelled to spread the word. For many years, I was a wandering preacher for this idea, arguing that this mathematics could, and should, be used to tackle scale. Meanwhile, students and staff were saying behind my back: Why work on code that will never be that efficient? Why are you wasting a promising career in theoretical computer science?

That's more or less how I ended up as one of the key people trying to solve the *scaling trilemma* discussed in the previous chapter.

Even prior to the Bitcoin conference, my ever-patient wife was tired of hearing about validity proofs, about interactive proofs (IP), about probabilistically checkable proofs (PCPs), and about zero-knowledge proofs (ZKPs). My students and colleagues were skeptical about my attempts to implement them in code, an effort I started several years earlier. The theoretical side was hot, but no one believed it could work in practice, nor could they find any interesting use cases. Yet deep down, I had a hunch that they might somehow be relevant in the "real world."

I described in an earlier chapter the lavishness and "unacademicness" of the 2013 conference. I had arrived ready to present the kind of talk I'd normally give in a university setting—rigorous, theoretical, and carefully argued. But the atmosphere at the conference was so different that I had to change course, or it would have been like having a bake sale at a rave.

So I scrapped the talk. In a slight panic, I opened my laptop and rewrote it on the spot—less math jargon, more problems that mattered to Bitcoiners. I gave it a new title in my head, amputated most of the math formulas, and put in concrete use cases instead. For example, how could batching and validity proofs lift throughput—a fancy way of talking about how much "traffic" this blockchain can handle? How could throughput become so massive that you can intuitively use them to pay for your morning coffee? How could validity proofs compress actual verification so that someone running blockchain on a smartphone, known as a *light client*, could verify everything without needing to trust a central authority? I wanted to show how exchanges could prove their reserves without revealing exact balances and how privacy could improve without losing transparency—not just elegant math, but tools you could use on Monday morning.

After the talk, I was surprised by the reactions. Some of the same people I'd seen earlier—signing autographs, speaking from the main stage, drawing crowds—came up to me. They were not just being polite; they actually sounded excited, saying that what I was talking about was exactly what they'd been waiting for. Specifically, I remember speaking with Greg Maxwell, one of the most important Bitcoin core developers, and asking him if he really understood what validity proofs and ZK proofs each were, and whether he really needed them. He did understand, and in the following days even posted a few novel concrete use cases on Bitcoin messaging forums.

People assume I got excited about Bitcoin because the price was rising. I didn't. It was the fact that the idea landed and the research I was working on suddenly seemed relevant to that crowd, which got me into Bitcoin. Until then, my work had been beautiful but distant—something appreciated by academics, not demanded by builders. Now it had traction. It had urgency. People told me that my obscure research might be the solution to one of their most significant unsolved problems: *scaling without abandoning blockchain's core principles.*

Oddly, I wasn't quite sure where validity proofs would fit into Bitcoin. But something had shifted. For the first time, it felt like the ideas I'd been chasing for years might actually matter—beyond the seminar room, beyond the citation list. This elegant but seemingly-theoretical math might actually matter to the real world.

Validity proofs contain two mind-blowing surprises, with seemingly impossible implications: scale and privacy. I'll describe the scaling superpower in this chapter and reserve privacy for a later one.

Radical Math: Succinct Verification and Scale

You must have experienced, at least once, the frustration of doing a long manual calculation—to compute your taxes, solve a tough math homework problem—only to stare at the end result knowing you must have made an error, and then spending grueling hours trying to figure out where you omitted a digit, flipped a plus sign into a minus, or opened the brackets in the wrong way. Mathematicians spend days reviewing pages of such equations when they referee important works (I can't imagine how much time was spent checking the 129 pages of Andrew Wiles's proof of Fermat's Last Theorem.).

What if I told you that all this effort is needless? That you could verify the correctness of any mathematical proof—or any computation, no matter how long—just by writing it in a certain format with numbers, then flipping through and picking 10 single digits, running a simple calculation (like adding them up), and based on the result—whether it's even or odd—decide if the entire proof was correct or if there was a tiny error hidden inside?

It sounds impossible, yet it's true. When proofs are expressed in the right mathematical form, random sampling can be enough to verify the integrity of the whole computation. As long as the Prover—the party trying to convince the world that a mathematical statement is correct—writes down the proof using the right format, anyone (mathematician or lay person) can act as Verifier—using random coin tosses to sample a few digits from the proof and run a few short calculations to gain high certainty that the statement is correct, without retracing the whole proof.

This amazing phenomenon can now be applied to enormous amounts of computation that carry immense value, like a year's worth of Bitcoin transactions. There is a way to check the validity and integrity of all these numerous payments, down to the last digit, using a simple and efficient computational process.

When we talk about checking integrity, we don't mean verifying the inputs. We're not asking whether you actually bought a coffee or sent money to a friend—those are your choices, your data. What we mean is checking the adding up. Did the system process and total everything correctly? Was every cent accounted for? In today's digital world, we're constantly relying on others—platforms, apps, institutions—to do this basic arithmetic on our behalf. We trust that their systems add things up without error or manipulation. But what if we didn't have to trust? What if we could check the math itself—quickly, easily, and with mathematical certainty? That's the kind of integrity we're talking about.

The method I am talking about for checking huge numbers of transactions down to the last digit is known as succinct verification, and I was the first to realize that it is the only viable endgame for scaling blockchain. It allows us to verify the integrity of a huge amount of computation while staying true to blockchain's ideal of everyone-is-invited; it is what my colleagues and I have been working on theoretically, what I reduced to practice, and what turned out to be the best way to scale blockchains.

If this sounds abstract, think back to the printing room from this book's introduction. The device you held didn't check each bill one by one—it didn't need to. It captured the whole room in a single flash and told you everything was correct. That's what succinct verification makes possible. A green light not for envelopes, but for a year's worth of decentralized financial activity. Not by trusting the printer, but by trusting the proof.

From Theory to Practice

I love archaeology, and whenever I'm standing at an excavation, seeing layers of history laid out in front of me, I'm struck by how much math is like that. When I sit in my office, using the proofs I've developed, they rest on many earlier layers of research. Or, as the cliche goes, we're doing so standing on the shoulders of giants.

The foundations on which my own innovations were built go back as far as the Pythagoreans in Greece thousands of years ago but I'm going to start in the early 1990s. László Babai, Lance Fortnow, Leonid A. Levin, and Mario Szegedy[1] showed that it was possible, in principle, to check massive computations using only a tiny amount of effort—thanks to clever encodings and interactive proofs. (A different team of researchers—Sanjeev Arora, Carsten Lund, Rajeev Motwani, Muli Safra, Madhu Sudan, and Mario Szegedy[2]—showed that the number of digits needed to be read from a proof is ridiculously small and even completely independent from the length of the proof or computation being verified.)

Babai et al. showed that you could check whether any computation was done correctly exponentially faster than it would take to check each and every step of it. Think of it as one careful PC supervising a herd of supercomputers running flaky or untested code. Let me show you the exact quote from their paper that stuck with me:

> . . .a single reliable PC can monitor the operation of a herd of supercomputers working with possibly extremely powerful but unreliable software and untested hardware.

A herd of supercomputers—like a herd of cattle—follows orders, but doesn't think for itself. In their example, the verifier is a careful checker—watching, questioning, smart enough to catch mistakes. The verifier (the PC) doesn't re-run the computation; the provers (the supercomputers) do the heavy work, and the verifier uses structured spot-checks to test consistency.

When I read this, my mind went to Archimedes. His lever is a simple physical idea with a massive implication. Archimedes figured out that with a long enough lever and the right pivot point, a small force can move the hugest of weights. How much strength do you need to lift a load? From the time of Archimedes that's the wrong question. The right question is what structure do you need. He is said to have declared: "Give me a place to stand, and I will move the Earth." This was no mere bravado, it was a statement about leverage, about how arranged mechanics can turn modest effort into outsized power.

Validity proofs stir in me a similar feeling of excitement. They do what seems impossible, defying all intuition. Using validity proofs feels like moving the earth with your bare hands.

Here's why they are so magical and counter-intuitive:

In most settings, a computer can't check a computation "from the outside." To be confident the result is correct, it usually has to redo essentially the same work, step for step. This is needed because verification is basically retracing the computation's path. It's like walking a hiking trail again to confirm someone really reached the summit.

To someone trained in computer science, the idea of succinct verification initially feels wrong—not because it contradicts experience, but because it seems to clash with some of the field's deepest assumptions. Alan Turing, often called the father of computer science, had already shown in the 1930s that there are limits no computer can overcome. His famous "halting problem" captured the idea: for some questions about programs, no machine can give you the answer in advance. To know what a computation does, you have to actually run it. That boundary has shaped the way we think about software, verification, and trust ever since. And yet, there are familiar situations—outside of computer science—where we accept exactly this kind of shortcut without thinking twice.

Think of a courtroom: A stenographer captures every word over several days. During cross-examination, lawyers don't replay the whole record; they pick a few precise questions anchored in the transcript to test credibility. If the answers contradict the transcript, the account is suspect.

Validity proofs work the same way. By prover, we mean the party that actually ran the full computation. Like the stenographer, the prover must still produce the equivalent of the complete court transcript. An encoded form of this transcript then becomes the proof—which is often even longer than the computation.

By verifier, we mean the checker. The verifier doesn't reread the entire transcript nor does it rerun the computation. Instead, it uses carefully designed mathematical tools and samples small, well-chosen parts of the proof and checks them for consistency. Because the proof is structured in a special way, this sampling would almost certainly catch even a single falsified part—just as a single contradiction in cross-examination can call an entire testimony into question.

So from the verifier's point of view, the process is efficient and trustworthy. The verifier can be sure the computation was carried out correctly, without re-running it and without relying on the prover's honesty. It looks like magic because verification is done exponentially faster than re-executing. It's like magically hopping in 10 steps from the head of the hiking trail to the summit that is miles away just because some earlier hiker (the prover) carefully trod a path.

I mentioned earlier that I used "magic" in this chapter's title on purpose. We both know what makes something feel like magic: it seems impossible, but there's always an explanation. That's exactly what's going on here. Turing's mathematics isn't being broken or bypassed. To explain why, let's go back to the hiking analogy.

Every step of the full hike is still being walked. The prover is the one doing that work—walking every step of the trail, all the way to the summit, and recording the journey in detail.

What changes is the burden on the verifier, the checker. The verifier doesn't need to retrace the entire hike. A few carefully chosen random questions suffice. It asks the equivalent of detailed questions about landmarks, turns, elevations, and their interconnectedness—things only someone who truly walked the path could answer consistently. Because of how the proof is constructed, those spot-checks are enough to confirm that the hiker walked the whole journey, with only a tiny fraction of the effort.

The prover and verifier together end up doing at least as much total work as just running the computation directly—sometimes more. What's different is how the work is split and how the two interact.

The prover does the heavy lifting, running the computation and producing a detailed proof. Once the proof is created, the prover commits to it—it can't be changed or withdrawn. The verifier then checks a few randomly chosen parts of that proof. Instead of redoing everything, the verifier uses a small number of smart, structured checks to confirm that the whole thing is valid.

This is where the magic comes in: interaction between the prover and verifier, and the randomness used by the verifier. Remove either one, and the whole thing falls apart.

These randomly guided checks are what make succinct proofs possible. STARKs—Scalable Transparent ARguments of Knowledge—bring this magic into the real world: they let us prove large computations with tiny proofs, no shortcuts, and no need for trusted setup. It's a way of saying nobody holds cryptographic master keys.

STARKs are the proof systems I'm most closely associated with. I co-invented them, and founded StarkWare to bring them from theory into real-world use—a mission that, as we'll see, is (pun intended) proving successful. STARKs, and systems like them, let us verify the correctness of a computation without redoing the work and without needing to blindly trust whoever ran it. They reflect a profound shift in how we think about trust in computation.

One Lever for Trust

When Archimedes said that, given a place to stand, he could move the Earth, he was making a claim about leverage, not strength. The same idea applies here. Validity proofs give us a way to apply a small amount of trusted effort at exactly the right point.

My Eureka at the 2013 Bitcoin conference was similar. A thought that's stuck with me since then is: "Give me a slow, weak, but trusted blockchain, and we'll enforce integrity on all computations on Earth." Archimedes, digital style.

In other words, if we had even a sluggish, costly platform—one that sticks to the everyone-is-invited principle and can run the math needed to verify validity proofs—we could use it to anchor global integrity.

In practical terms, this means that a slow, expensive, but trusted system—a blockchain—can be used to enforce integrity over vast amounts of computation performed elsewhere. The blockchain doesn't do the work itself. It acts as the fixed point. The lever is the proof.

The result is that even the very largest actors in the world today—corporations, monopolies, or nation-states—are unable to slip false computations past the public system without being caught. There is absolutely no practical way to forge a proof that passes the verifier's checks. Any person who has a laptop or smartphone could run that tiny verification and help keep the world honest.

Why Succinct Verification Works

At its core, succinct verification is a way to check that a massive computation was carried out correctly—without repeating all the work yourself.

To see why this works, think about statistical polling: using small random samples to draw reliable conclusions about a large whole. Polling and statistics work incredibly well, and we make use of them everywhere. When a lab test is run, it uses random sampling. When we give a blood or urine sample, a drop is taken and processed—yet we trust that the results reflect our true glucose or urea levels. Why is this so? Because the laws of math and statistics suggest that it's nearly impossible for your true blood glucose level to be 90, but one single drop to be 100. The odds of this happening are similar to the odds of mixing a cup of tea, stirring it, and finding that the upper left section is completely clear water, void of tea particles. In both cases, the odds are lower than the chance that a dinosaur-killing-sized meteor hits Earth as you're reading this book.

This is hard stuff, so here's another way to picture it. You arrive at a public swimming pool, just as a group of 200 toddlers is leaving.

You do the math in your head: What are the odds none of them had a little accident? Are we entering a Code Brown biohazard environment? Nobody wants to swim in water contaminated by poop germs—but testing every drop is impossible.

So the pool staff run a chemical test, adding a few drops of solution to a sample of pool water. It changes color if there's any contamination. They don't need to test the whole pool since the solution is so sensitive it picks up even the tiniest trace.

Validity proofs work in a very similar way—but for big computer tasks. If someone changes even a single digit in a computation—like slipping in an extra zero—this can quietly inflate balances or redirect value, allowing someone to steal money or manipulate outcomes while making the final result look legitimate. It is so easy for such a thing to go unnoticed. But a validity proof verifier will catch it. Like the poop test. And here's the mind-bending part: It can do this by randomly sampling a few computational "drops" (not even a full line of the computation).

The prover produces the detailed proof, and the verifier is the staff member who sampled the water. If anything was done wrong, the proof will almost certainly fail. Adding the proof to the blockchain is the equivalent of pinning the "proof drops" of water on the pool notice board.

Why Succinct Verification Suddenly Mattered in 2013

By 2013, succinct verification had been a theoretical idea for decades; Bitcoin made its relevance obvious. For years, the idea of succinct validity proofs was largely a mathematical curiosity. We knew it had theoretical value, but practical uses were few and far between. Then blockchain came along—and the relevance snapped into focus.

Today, there is an entire industry built around the power of these proofs. Seeing that happen—having run ahead of the crowd and put my reputation on the line to help trigger these moves—is deeply gratifying. It is also gratifying to have lived two lives: first as the mathematician formulating the research, and now, in my current role, as the CEO of the multibillion-dollar company that has led this movement.

Blockchains require every node to rerun each transaction, like having every bank clerk recalculate your balance. That's a huge task. But what if a single cryptographic proof could validate the entire batch?

Rather than log each transaction, you generate one proof that covers a whole batch at once. The math ensures that if just one transaction in that batch were dishonest, the proof would fail. It's fast, compact, and—most importantly—tamper-proof.

And being tamper-proof changes everything. Because once something hits the blockchain, it's there for good. Every transaction that precedes it needs to be correct before it can be added. It's like submitting a financial statement to be etched in stone: You need to be absolutely sure it checks out.

Succinct validity proofs serve as fast pre-screeners—verifying all calculations with a single, compact proof. They reduce load, increase capacity, and boost security. And in doing so, they make blockchains scalable. That was the "A-ha" moment.

Like many other breakthroughs, this one, as I write, is being transformed into life-changing, real-world technology. A multibillion-dollar company has been built from it, and it's pushing the boundaries of what's possible. But before I get into the details of my dramatic story, let me give a glimpse into what validity proofs can do on a mass scale. After all, we aren't just building; we're building for humanity.

CHAPTER 9

Infrastructure for the Unbanked

In the last chapter, we discussed the concept of scale and the thrill and promise of building blockchain's capacity. Who needs it? The simple answer—and the central argument of this book—is that everyone does. But I don't mean the traders and the technomic (tech plus economy) elites. I mean, everyone, the whole world. To understand this, let's jump into why blockchain is more than a project of the privileged.

Many people, especially those blessed with an investment bank account and a stable currency, make the mistake of dismissing blockchain as overblown, a hammer desperately seeking a nail. They don't expect financial institutions to fail; they've never had their account closed or a payment frozen. And yet, even for the well-heeled, everyday frictions feel familiar, whether it's being told you can transfer only a limited amount of cash, despite having sufficient funds, or being asked to fill out endless forms. These may seem like mere minor inconveniences, but they are actually reminders that access is conditional and restricted.

Meanwhile, there are 1.4 billion people around the world who still don't have access to a bank account. For them, blockchain represents an entry ticket to the modern world. Without it, they're on the sidelines. With it, they have instant access to an infrastructure for finance and more that is open to all and from which no one can exclude them.

The irony is that, in a world where millions still lack bank accounts, the internet has spawned a global economy of "gig workers." They tag data and moderate content online, but receive payment by cash or by gift cards because there's no established banking system. That's not just inefficient. It's unjust.

We've already seen that blockchain isn't just about money; it's also a system for record-keeping, coordination, and new kinds of trust. This chapter begins with payments and savings—the financial uses of blockchain—and then turns to non-financial applications such as identity, provenance, and coordination.

The Boy Who Harnessed the Wind

If you want a 90-minute, Hollywood-style insight into how removing even one small barrier can mean the difference between despair and survival, watch the movie *The Boy Who Harnessed the Wind*. It's the true story of William Kamkwamba, who was just 14 when his village, Wimbe, in Malawi, was gripped by famine.

Prospects were dire, and people were already dying. William chanced upon a library book about windmills and built one himself, from tractor parts, broken bicycles, and branches. The windmill powered a pump, bringing water to the fields and ultimately food to the table. Without that spark of innovation, his family—and his community—were facing starvation, with no path forward. What changed their fate wasn't aid from above, but resourcefulness in the face of hardship.

Not everyone experiences such serendipity. Not everyone can find the right book and the right spark of initiative to put together scraps and change lives. Not everyone can build a windmill. But you don't need serendipity to stumble on blockchain, and you don't need unique talents to use it. Blockchain can deliver the same leap Kamkwamba's windmill did, turning outsiders into participants and exclusion into inclusion.

What William Kamkwamba gave his village wasn't abstract hope; it was a concrete tool. Blockchain too is a concrete tool that can change lives. It provides an entry ticket for those on the sidelines. The villagers of Wimbe had no rain, no harvest, and no money for school. The parallel with blockchain is clear. The windmill was a physical tool. Blockchain is a digital tool. It provides people with a means of entry into the global economy. Today, through blockchain,

I can interact with someone I've never met, not as an act of charity, but as part of a mutually beneficial, verifiable system. That's not utopian. That's infrastructure.

To ground this in a real context, consider one region where these needs are especially vivid: Africa.

Blockchain in Africa

From cross-border payments for freelancers to remittances that settle in minutes and cooperatives that use on-chain records for transparency, blockchain technology is most powerful where it meets real needs and skips past legacy systems. These realities show why Africa needs blockchain, and, just as importantly, why blockchain needs Africa. Africa is full of places where creativity flourishes despite constraint, where people already think beyond what's broken and leapfrog what's missing. In that way, the continent is not behind—it's ahead.

That's why, in the year after StarkWare reached a multibillion-dollar valuation, we created a dedicated effort focused on Africa—to collaborate with local builders, to support ventures that solve real problems, and to learn where technology meets the most pressing human needs. For blockchain to grow with integrity and purpose, it must be shaped by those who know firsthand the costs of exclusion.

In parts of Africa, blockchain isn't a buzzword. It's a solution.

A student in Nairobi, Kenya, finishes a freelance job for a client in London. The money comes in dollars—sometimes via a stablecoin, sometimes not. She needs shillings. Not someday—today. Rent is due. Her brother needs school supplies. However, she doesn't have a bank account, and even if she did, the exchange rates between currencies are unreliable—too many forms; too much waiting. So she swaps currency peer-to-peer. She messages someone she trusts—or someone the trusted person trusts—who has what she needs. They meet. They trade. It's not smooth, but it works.

In Lagos, Nigeria, another worker moderates online content. They review posts, flag disinformation, and work through moderation queues. It pays, but not in naira. The platform sends gift cards by way of payment. That's the most "universal" option they can offer. So the worker takes the cards and finds a way to convert them.

Maybe to cash. Maybe to airtime. Maybe to crypto, if they're lucky enough to know the right channel. None of this is sanctioned. All of it is necessary.

In Zambia, a hydrostation hums quietly beside a river. It powers a village and still has energy left over. There's no grid to feed it into. No utility company to buy the surplus. So instead, the excess energy powers a few machines that are mining Bitcoin. It's not flashy. The earnings aren't huge. But it's better than nothing and the energy would otherwise go to waste.

In places where mobile data is expensive or unreliable, people find fixes. One household gets a connection—maybe through a mobile router, maybe something cobbled together—and shares it with the neighbors. No contract. No company support. Just a signal that reaches their kitchen table.

To keep things fair, they use software built on blockchain to keep a tally of who's online, how much they've used, and what they owe. A few cents at a time. Enough to keep the system running.

It's not perfect. But it works. Most of the time, that's enough.

This isn't some future use case. It's now. Students, freelancers, small business owners—people who've never heard of consensus algorithms or zero-knowledge proofs—are already relying on these systems. Not because they're ideal, but because they're better than being stuck.

No one's trying to make a point. They're just trying to get paid. To move money. To stay connected. No one needs to call it blockchain, but it happens to be the rails underneath these everyday transactions.

Global Remittance Corridors

I started this book with a claim: that in the future, the internet and blockchain will be indistinguishable. The cross-border online labor market is where that convergence is clearest.

Consider the global remittance corridors—the most-traveled routes for migrants sending money home (e.g., New York to Lagos/Dubai to Dhaka). Today, that journey is expensive and slow: a fee here, a delay there, compliance checks and bank "de-risking" that exclude smaller senders, and long lines for cash-out at the last mile.

Infrastructure for the Unbanked

Billions of dollars are lost each year to inefficiency. With blockchain, that path gets shorter. Using blockchain rails, stablecoins can settle value in minutes; local on/off ramps deliver to mobile money or bank accounts; and transparent, programmable compliance reduces friction. No one asks where you bank or how you prove your address. It just works.

Or take the growing ranks of freelancers and creators across the world—editing videos, labeling data, writing code. Platforms connect them to clients, but often stumble when it's time to pay. Some get frozen out entirely, flagged as "high risk" just for being where they are. Others wait weeks for cross-border wires to clear. Meanwhile, in another corner of the world, a journalist manages to evade government surveillance. Financial cut-offs can't censor their reporting because they are funded through crypto. Not because it's cool, but because it's the only option left.

And sometimes the problem isn't just friction; it's shutdown. When economies wobble or governments clamp down, banks impose capital controls, withdrawal limits, and foreign exchange bans. Argentines know the *cepo cambiario* (foreign currency restrictions) all too well; in Turkey, rules on foreign-currency transfers can change overnight; in Russia and Ukraine, war and sanctions have blocked transfers and frozen accounts. At times like these, the banking rails don't just creak—they vanish. Crypto becomes the lifeboat.

Blockchain doesn't fix everything. But it does fix the payout bottleneck. It makes payment native to the network. Fast, direct, uncensorable. It completes the loop. It's a contemporary answer to a need that is so old that it's discussed in the Bible. Wages must be paid "each day before sunset"—not via gift cards or the promise of payment someday.

I often use a debit card tied to a self-custodial crypto wallet—a wallet that I truly own, like I own cash in my pocket or a ring on my hand, and in a better way than I "own" a bank deposit (the bank holds the deposit and I need its authorization to spend it). With this crypto-backed debit card, I can spend funds drawn directly from crypto stored on the blockchain—no exchange or intermediary involved. The funds are automatically converted as needed from crypto to dollars or euros, and transferred there in two seconds, not three days as typical when using a bank. There are no surprise phone calls to justify a payment, no paper forms, no arbitrary transfer caps despite having funds, and no "office hours" where doors shut on evenings or weekends. Payments move at 2 a.m. on a Sunday just as they move at noon on a Tuesday.

It's a small everyday example of why permissionless rails—open networks anyone can use without a gatekeeper's approval—matter: They reduce friction for the well-banked and keep that door open for those who are unbanked.

CHAPTER 10

Blockchain in Practice: Usability, Scaling, and Privacy

In previous chapters, we talked about why the world needs blockchain; we also examined the math that enables blockchain. We'll now see how my math story became part of the real-world story.

We are going to be exploring the following three points, which will anchor the rest of this chapter:

1. Blockchain should be safe and simple for daily use, but today's infrastructure cannot handle mainstream volume.
2. Blockchain should function at scale, serving billions of people. But we need to be careful how we solve the scaling problem so that we don't recreate the same old centralized chokepoints—this is the *decentralization-security-scalability trilemma* (otherwise known as the *scaling* or *tricky trilemma*), which we covered earlier in the book. The challenge is to square the impossible-sounding circle: stay decentralized, stay secure, and still scale.
3. Blockchain's potential in terms of what it can do goes way beyond the digital currency dreams of Bitcoin and Ethereum. Blockchain can embed privacy-preserving mechanisms directly into the base protocol without adding trusted intermediaries (e.g., using zero-knowledge proofs).

Now, let's go back in time to that 2013 Bitcoin conference, when I finally realized that the work I'd been doing for intellectual joy might actually have a practical purpose. Math, like validity proofs that once lived quietly in seminar rooms, suddenly had a job to do. It was no longer about impressing peer-reviewing professors who had the power to publish or spike my research. It was about moving money, safeguarding votes, protecting privacy, and letting people collaborate across borders without trusting a black box.

You need more than principles to pay workers on a public, global network. You need proofs—fast, compact, and verifiable at scale—that can also protect privacy. That realization is what sent me back to the 2013 Bitcoin conference.

At the time of the conference, I was partway through a two-year sabbatical, first at Microsoft Research and then at MIT. It was meant to be a time for reflection, for deep work. And it was then that I decided to explore the commercial opportunities for my research. My biggest passion was, and still is, scaling blockchain to mass usage through math and validity proofs. But my first entry into blockchain entrepreneurship was through the second benefit of these proofs: privacy and zero knowledge.

Radical Math: Zero-Knowledge Privacy

Validity proofs deliver two benefits: scale and privacy. First, they allow multiple transactions to be bundled into a single, compact proof that can be quickly verified by the network—that's scale. Second, the zero-knowledge variant of validity proofs proves correctness without revealing any transaction details—that's privacy. We can choose to use the proofs at different times for their scaling benefits, their privacy benefits, or both. Having covered scale in a previous chapter, we now turn to privacy.

The radical idea I'm describing now is that you can create a convincing proof that a given statement is true without revealing anything about the content of the proof itself. The only thing people learn is that the statement is true. For mathematicians, the proof is often more important than the statement. Take Fermat's Last Theorem. It remained unproven for over 350 years until British mathematician Andrew Wiles completed a brilliant proof in 1994, building on centuries of prior work. What mattered wasn't just that the theorem was true—it was the fact that it could finally be proven. Now imagine a twist: we're all convinced Wiles has proved the theorem, but he doesn't show us how. We don't see a single step. Instead, he locks his proof in a box, seals it cryptographically, and hands us a compact digital certificate that convinces us the proof exists and is correct. That's the idea.

A zero-knowledge proof—abbreviated "ZK proof" (also written "ZK")—is a cryptographic proof that convinces a verifier a statement is true while revealing nothing else about the underlying data. The magical, counterintuitive thing about zero-knowledge proofs is that you are convinced beyond any reasonable doubt that a statement (or theorem) is true, but the proof provides you with no knowledge whatsoever about its content.

Here is how you could use ZK. Imagine your daughter, niece, or a close friend—a 21-year-old woman out alone at night, safety-conscious and a little uneasy. All she wants is to buy a bottle of wine. But to do that, she's expected to hand over an ID that shows not just her age, but her full name and home address. She hesitates. Why should a stranger across the counter need to know where she lives?

Zero-knowledge (ZK) proofs aren't just for highfalutin finance. They apply to situations like this too.

Instead of providing the ID to the wine seller, you have your phone generate a ZK proof that (a) the birthdate is signed by the issuer and (b) your birthdate was at least 21 years ago. You present only the proof and the issuer's public key—the widely shared key used to verify the issuer's signature. The clerk verifies the proof; no birthdate, address, or other details are revealed. The ZK proof proves only what's needed—and nothing more.

How Zero-Knowledge Proofs Work

Here's another simple example of a zero-knowledge proof: Think of a four-digit combination lock. Suppose you know the combination that opens the lock—let's say it's 2315—and you want to prove to me that you know it. The simplest way is for you to tell me the combination and let me check. But by doing so, you're revealing more than you need to—not just that you know the combination, but the additional (and unnecessary) information that the number is 2315. You've gone beyond your original statement, "I know the combination to open this lock," and you've revealed the actual combination.

So let's consider a different proof. Same result—I'm convinced you know the combination, but you don't reveal the actual digits. Here's how: You take the lock, turn around so I don't see, and open it. You then show me the open lock while hiding the combination with your hand. You know the combination is 2315. I have no clue what it is. But what I do know, beyond question, is that you know the combination. You can unlock it again and again, and I still won't know the combination.

Zero-knowledge proofs work like that. The prover uses their knowledge to convince the verifier that they have a proof of a mathematical statement. The prover manages to convince the verifier that the mathematical statement (say, Fermat's Last Theorem) is true and valid, but the verifier learns nothing beyond the validity of the statement.

The example about the combination lock makes zero-knowledge proofs seem easy; we can readily imagine the proof explained there. But the real shocker, the real magic about zero-knowledge proofs, is that they work not just with locks, but with any mathematical statement or computation.

I'd like you to pause for a moment and try to find a way to prove the correctness of any theorem—for example, the infinity of prime numbers (however big a prime number is, there's always one bigger). Think about how you'd convince someone else the theorem is correct, without revealing any additional information.

Now take something more playful. Suppose you've solved a Sudoku puzzle. Can you convince me you have the right solution—without showing me the answer?

To prove any mathematical statement without revealing anything about your proof method, there has to be some magical (i.e., mathematical) way to convert the statement and its proof into a game between the two of us: You demonstrate that you can consistently "open the lock" without ever revealing the secret itself. That's what we mean by interactive—not a one-time reveal, but a back-and-forth. The verifier (me) generates a series of cryptographic locks, each shaped slightly differently. The prover (you) responds by opening each one, convincingly, without exposing how you're doing it. Each round is a fresh challenge. And with every correct response, my confidence grows—not because I've learned your secret, but because I've seen you handle every lock I've thrown your way.

It's actually far less abstract than it sounds. It's exactly how relationships work. We might say things like "I looked in her eyes and saw her soul," but in truth, we fall in love—and decide to spend our lives with someone—after seeing how they respond to different situations over time. That's what dating is for. We watch them under pressure, in joy, in conflict, in kindness. And slowly, something in us says: I trust this person. I adore them. It's not one moment. It's the pattern.

From Controversy to Acceptance

So far, we defined zero-knowledge proofs, explained why they matter, and showed how they enable trust without exposure. But it's important to understand what a huge impact they had when the world first understood what they were. Accepting them as "proofs" took some time.

Mathematicians are a conservative bunch. The idea that a "proof" could be an interactive process between two parties made mathematicians uneasy. And many pushed against the fact that ZK proofs have a tiny speck of imperfection in that there is a minuscule chance that a false statement could be accepted as true—far less probability-wise than winning the lottery dozens of times in a row, but still a chance. Even within the field of cryptography and theoretical computer science, it took time for these proofs to be accepted as important and interesting. The paper[1] that introduced zero-knowledge proofs—by Shafi Goldwasser, Silvio Micali, and Charles Rackoff—was reportedly rejected four times from top peer-reviewed venues before being accepted and adopted as a breakthrough in cryptography worthy of the highest awards in our field.

Once this was accepted, professionals and some laypeople alike understood the importance of zero-knowledge proofs. *The New York Times* ran the front-page headline "A New Approach to Protecting Secrets" in February 1987, when it reported on the breakthrough giving some mainstream recognition to Goldwasser, Micali, and

Rackoff. Their zero-knowledge proofs could revolutionize secure identification and authentication processes across the world, said reporter James Gleick. His article captured the paradox at the heart of the discovery: a way to prove that you know a thing exists—without revealing the thing itself. "You want to be able to prove some fact and not disclose why the fact is true," said Micali of MIT. "You want to convince without giving more knowledge than is strictly necessary."[2] That line stuck with me. It reshaped how I understood proofs—not as full disclosures, but as targeted guarantees.

To recap once again to be sure we are on the same page: In a ZK proof, a prover convinces a verifier that a claim is true while revealing no additional information. One party, you (the prover), convinces another, me (the verifier), that a claim is true. Crucially, I learn nothing beyond that truth. Not the reasoning. Not the data. Just the certainty.

The elegance of ZK proofs lies in these three defining properties:

1. *Completeness:* If the claim is true, the verifier will be convinced.
2. *Soundness:* If the claim is false, no cheating prover can succeed—or rather, the chance that a cheater could succeed is smaller than the chance of a cosmic ray flipping every bit in your computer at once. In plain terms: The odds of being fooled are astronomically low.
3. *Zero-knowledge:* The verifier learns nothing they can reuse. Nothing that leaks. That's the point.

Goldwasser, Micali, and Rackoff introduced the foundations of zero-knowledge and interactive proofs in the mid-1980s. Around the same time, Micali, together with Oded Goldreich and Avi Wigderson, showed how to build ZK proofs for any efficiently verifiable statement.[3]

What was theoretical is now practical. Modern proof systems make ZK fast and scalable in real deployments.

This story has personal resonance. For years, I worked on these kinds of proofs without much attention beyond academia. Then blockchain emerged—and suddenly, the world needed what we had, not as a curiosity, but as essential scaling infrastructure.

And the story comes full circle. Shafi Goldwasser and my PhD advisor Avi Wigderson, both recipients of the Turing Award, the mathematics equivalent of a Nobel Prize, which they were awarded in honor of their work in cryptography and theoretical computer science, have since joined StarkWare as scientific advisors. For me, that's more than an endorsement. It's a generational handoff from an early innovator.

We are building on foundations laid by giants, pushing forward a vision that once lived only in theory, but is now coming to life at scale.

From "Galactic" Proofs to Practical Systems

Many improvements were made to early validity proofs in the 1990s, in terms of both scale and privacy, but it would be another 30 years before they appeared as part of a mass-use product. There are two reasons for this delay. The first is that the best-use case for them—blockchain—didn't exist until 2008. But the second reason is that early versions were what mathematicians call *galactic algorithms*—theoretically innovative but impractical.

The term *galactic algorithm* was coined by theoretical computer scientists Richard Lipton and Ken Regan, both from the United States, to describe algorithms and methods that are provably better than what we use today on our computers—but only for problems so vast they would require all the atoms in our galaxy to even describe them. Until roughly the end of the 2000s, zero-knowledge and validity proofs were considered galactic algorithms.

At that time, the early validity-proof constructions seemed hopeless. How do I know? Years later, after STARKs were already in production, I gave a talk at the Hebrew University in Jerusalem. I spoke to Michael Ben-Or, a famous theoretical computer science professor there, who told me he'd looked into validity proofs back in the 1990s. Big problems require impossible computing power, as we've just seen. But he was trying to see if there was a problem that was small enough that its correctness could be checked by succinct verification methods using the hardware of the day. The answer was a resounding no.

He concluded that no combination of computers that existed then or in the foreseeable future would ever be able to generate a proof for such a problem. That's even accounting for Moore's Law—the prediction that computing power doubles roughly every two years. The electricity and disk space needed would be prohibitive, he said.

But we never say never. The late 2000s and early 2010s saw remarkable progress. A number of breakthroughs transformed the landscape and made succinct verification and zero-knowledge practical. At the time I was working on probabilistically checkable proofs (PCPs). PCPs gave the idea: A verifier can spot-check a long proof and still be confident. In the late 2000s and early 2010s, cryptographers turned that idea into practical systems.

This line of research started with an assumption that the PCP technology I was working on speeding up, in spite of being highly secure, was not efficient. Disproving this assumption, and showing that PCP-based proofs are not only more secure, but also more efficient, is one of the academic accomplishments I'm most proud of (and the focus of the next chapter).

To make progress without the needed mathematical breakthroughs, researchers suggested bringing more cryptography to bear. Researchers proposed replacing the most complex pieces of PCPs with elliptic-curve cryptography (ECC). The result was a new family of proofs called *ZK-SNARKs*, which make zero-knowledge possible without heavy computation. In 2012, Rosario Gennaro, Craig Gentry, Bryan Parno, and Mariana Raykova (GGPR) built the first practical ZK-SNARK system efficient enough for real deployment.[4]

ZK-SNARKs

The elegant and snarky elliptic-curve-based constructions, aptly called *ZK-SNARKs*, addressed a major shortcoming in the best cryptography of the time, and created something new. The GGPR construction (which takes its name from the initials of the four co-authors mentioned above) was a breakthrough—it was the first time that some ZK construction could be built for general-purpose computation. But it worked only for very simple programs—fixed "circuits" with no loops, no memory, and no way to react to changing input. That made it too limited for real software.

In 2013 I published a paper titled "SNARKs for C,"[5] together with Tel Aviv University faculty member Eran Tromer and PhD students from MIT and Technion Alessandro Chiesa, Daniel Genkin, and Madars Virza. It was built on GGPR but removed its biggest limitation: It could now handle full, general-purpose programs, including those that use memory and make decisions. C is one of the most widely used programming languages in the world. It powers operating systems, databases, and even the small "brains" inside everyday devices. By supporting C, our system was no longer just theory—it could prove the correctness of code people actually use. For the first time, you could imagine writing normal code in C and generating a short cryptographic proof that the output was correct. The proofs were tiny, just a few hundred bytes, and could be checked in milliseconds.

ZK-SNARKs had started as an academic idea. By this point, they were ready to be tried and tested in real protocols for privacy applications.

Zerocash: A ZK-SNARK-Based Private Payments Protocol

One year after our ZK-SNARK paper, my team partnered with Johns Hopkins' researcher Matt Green and his students Christina Garman and Ian Miers. Their 2013 work, "Zerocoin[6]," proposed bolstering Bitcoin's privacy using a technology that is less powerful than STARKs/SNARKs, called RSA accumulators. Our collaboration produced *Zerocash*, a protocol that uses ZK-SNARKs to provide end-to-end private payments—not an add-on to Bitcoin, but a full shielded-transaction system. We formalized this in the paper titled "Zerocash."[7]

Bitcoin, for all its benefits, has a glaring flaw—it is transparent to a fault. Every transaction is out in the open: who sent it, who received it, and for how much. That's fine for auditability, but terrible for privacy. The Zerocash protocol flipped the model. We wanted people to transact securely, but without broadcasting their business to the world.

We built the tools to make that possible. Using the SNARKs we'd developed the year before, we enabled users to create a transaction and submit a cryptographic proof that it was valid—that it followed all the protocol rules—without revealing any of the actual transaction data. The blockchain would accept the proof, verify it in milliseconds, and move on.

Zerocash marked a fundamental shift. It was the first real-world use of zero-knowledge proofs for general-purpose computation—as opposed to just isolated facts such as proving you know a password, but for an entire system of financial transactions. "General-purpose" here means that the zero-knowledge proof wasn't hardcoded for a single task. Instead, it could represent a wide range of transaction logic—who paid whom, how much, and when—without revealing any of those details. Zcash, which implemented the Zerocash protocol, brought this to life. For the first time, users could move real money on a public blockchain while keeping amounts and addresses fully private—thanks to zero-knowledge proofs. This wasn't a niche tool; it was a full privacy-preserving payment system, live and operational in the wild.

No need to see the sender, receiver, or amount. The network could be sure that the rules were followed without knowing who was playing the game.

For example, say Alice wants to pay Bob privately. The app on her smartphone (her wallet) generates a tiny SNARK proving that she (1) controls the funds and has digitally signed the transaction, (2) the funds are unspent and sufficient, and (3) the amounts balance once the fee is included. All of this takes place without revealing who's paying whom or how much.

Alice's wallet sends a cryptographic proof that the transaction is valid (known as *broadcasting*) to the nodes (the computers on the network that check it). After the transaction is verified using its SNARK proof, it gets included in the next block on the blockchain.

Bob's wallet (holding his secret key) recognizes the incoming payment and notifies him as soon as it's confirmed. Everything is encrypted, including the amount and the recipient. So if Alice made two payments from the same address, there'd be nothing to connect them—preserving her financial privacy and identity.

With Zerocash we showed this wasn't just an idea—it was a working system. We wrote the academic paper and built the prototype. It proved that privacy and trust didn't have to be polar opposites. You could have both. I remember describing it later as "the first system that allows people to use a cryptocurrency, but without anyone being able to trace the origin, the destination, or the amount of a payment." For me and many others, it was the moment when this arc of mathematical research, the privacy aspect of validity proofs, touched the real world.

We shifted paths and joined forces with a brilliant and visionary entrepreneur, Zooko Wilcox-O'Hearn, and his team of cyberpunk engineers to co-found the Electric Coin Company and launch Zcash as an independent cryptocurrency.

Zerocash, the research project, became Zcash, the cryptocurrency, protecting its users' privacy with ZK-SNARKs. We're very proud of Zcash—but we've always wanted, and still want, Bitcoin to use our zero-knowledge proofs. To this very day, I hope they'll adopt the technology, but I recognize it may take a long time. We're writing this book 12 years after ZK-SNARKs, and there's still only a glimmer of hope. But I'm convinced the day will arrive, and I'm working hard to make it happen.

To launch Zcash, we needed one more step: a one-time trusted setup to generate the SNARK public parameters.

The Ceremony: Trusted Setup for ZK-SNARKs

Before Zcash launched, its ZK-SNARK system required a one-time "trusted setup" to create public parameters. Participants ran a multi-party computation, each adding unique cryptographic secrets. The process produced a proving key and a verification key, but also a dangerous byproduct: if the participants' secrets were later recovered and combined, they would form the cryptographic equivalent of a master key. This "toxic waste" would allow an attacker to forge proofs. Security depended on participants destroying their secrets; if even one person deleted theirs, the system was safe. However, if everyone colluded and kept their waste, they could reconstruct that secret access to withdraw funds or corrupt the system at will.

In 2016, Zooko coordinated a global event dubbed the "Ceremony" to run this setup for Zcash. Participants on several continents contributed randomness, generated the keys, and destroyed their local data. It is called a *ceremony* because the carefully scripted, verifiable destruction of secrets serves as a public ritual of trust without a central authority.

By late 2016, Zcash had gone live. The system worked. It let users choose: Keep your transactions public, the same as on Bitcoin, or use *shielded addresses* that hide everything—sender, receiver, amount. *Shielded* meant the transaction data was encrypted on the blockchain, visible only to the parties involved, but still verifiable by the network.

The math behind it was tight. You could prove the transaction was valid without showing the details. For the first time, full privacy on a public blockchain wasn't just a theory. And in the beginning, it felt like we'd cracked something. Within days, ZEC (the coin of the Zcash network) was changing hands for thousands of dollars.

Why did the price of ZEC spike? Two reasons: excitement about private payments and a tiny circulating supply at launch (thin markets + new tech = wild prices). But adoption stalled just months after launch. The tech was there, but the tools weren't—meaning the practical infrastructure for regular users to access and use shielded transactions was still missing. Shielded transactions required more memory and bandwidth because the limits of small devices were stretched by the need to generate and verify the cryptographic proofs, which involved complex computations. The cryptocurrency exchanges didn't support z-addresses (the private addresses used for shielded transactions). So most people carried on using Zcash like Bitcoin, fully public. They missed out on its unique selling point.

Then came the pressure. Regulators got nervous. Some exchanges delisted the coin. Others never listed it at all. The ideals were still there. It had started as Zerocash—a vision for privacy in the open—but it did not grow into a mass movement.

Discovering STARKs

Despite the purpose of Zcash, one major thing held it back—in my mind, and in the minds of many cypherpunks: the trusted setup. Security depended on at least one participant permanently deleting their secret randomness. If any secret survived or was later recovered, an adversary could forge proofs and mint counterfeit Zcash without detection.

An understandable example of this problem is reading your credit card number to a call center that promises to delete it. If any copy remains, someone can charge the card later. In ZK-SNARKs, a leftover setup "secret" similarly lets someone forge proofs and effectively "print money."

That single assumption—that the trusted setup could truly be trusted forever—became the Achilles' heel of early ZK-SNARK systems, including Zcash's original design, and the reason the world looked for SNARK alternatives.

Even with careful procedures, these early ZK-SNARK systems rely on a trusted setup. If all the participants retained their secret randomness ("toxic waste"), they could collude to forge proofs and mint counterfeit ZEC. Because Bitcoin avoids trusted setups by design, adopting such a system is unlikely. Two risks follow from that setup assumption: an operational risk if any secret survives and a cryptographic risk from future advances.

To make things worse, a new threat to elliptic curve cryptography grows larger with every passing day: quantum computers. Governments and high-tech companies like Google, Microsoft, and IBM are pouring billions into the research and development of these machines. If even one of them reaches the scale predicted by theoretical physicists, the SNARKs used in Zcash and elsewhere would go extinct. That bothered me—not just because of the risk, but because I knew a better approach already existed—one that didn't rely on hidden assumptions. Just clean math, visible to all, with no back doors—and crucially, immune to the same quantum computers that would make such ZK-SNARKs obsolete.

The push to remove trusted setup using only hash functions and PCP encodings led to the cryptography I work with today: ZK-STARKs, or Integrity Express Take Two. ZK-STARKs not only removed the need for the Ceremony, but also offered a path to scale blockchain while preserving privacy, without sacrificing security or decentralization. And they are immune to attacks by quantum computers, which pose an ever-growing threat to Bitcoin and much of the internet's cryptographic infrastructure. With ZK-STARKs, I now had a robust and future proof tool to address both of the holy grails I'd been chasing since 2013—privacy and scaling.

The difference is simple. With SNARKs, if Darth Vader controlled the Ceremony, you were screwed. If a large-scale quantum computer shows up tomorrow, you're screwed. And if you ever need to handle bigger computations than the original parameters were sized for—unless you redo the Ceremony—you're not exactly screwed, but you're stuck. The system just won't scale any further.

With STARKs, none of these problems occur. Darth Vader could be building the very app you use to manage your funds and operate the fastest quantum computer there is, but he still couldn't get his hands on a penny. The system works efficiently and securely at any imaginable scale.

It sounds amazing, and it is—which is exactly why, almost as soon as I co-founded StarkWare to bring it into the real world, we had investors coming to us. And within a few years, we had an $8 billion valuation.

CHAPTER 11

Research Springs to Life: From Breakthrough to Blueprint

STARKs, the cryptography I described at the end of the previous chapter, hit the public in 2018, as an academic paper with the catchy title "Scalable, Transparent, and Post-Quantum Secure Computational Integrity."[1] There was no flashy launch video or press blitz. The paper, co-authored with my students Iddo Bentov, Yinon Horesh, and Michael Riabzev, was aimed at researchers, and it would be quite some time before most people in the blockchain community made use of STARKs.

Spoiler: Today, that same cryptography is at the heart of my company, StarkWare. And as I'll discuss in a later chapter, it is also being used by some of our fiercest competitors, among them RISC Zero, Polygon, zkSync, and Succinct. Whether friend, rival, or something in between, they are all helping to expand a technology that started life in my research notebooks.

I realize that some people like to read the story first and then delve into the details and some prefer the reverse, so I have prepared an appendix at the back of the book with some depth on STARKs for you to dip into as you wish.

What a Breakthrough Really Looks Like

People like to imagine breakthroughs as a single, dramatic moment—a lightning flash when the problem cracks wide open and the solution stands there, flawless, waiting to be written down. Archimedes leaps from his bath, rubber duck in hand, shouting, "Eureka!"

Some breakthroughs in my career did look like that, but others unfolded much more quietly and unexpectedly. The path leading to STARKs had a fair share of both.

I still remember the excitement back in 2003—an episode I first mentioned in the introduction and Chapter 8—when I thought we'd found a perfect way to get short validity proofs, called *probabilistically checkable proofs* (PCPs). They're a way to convince someone that a complex statement is true by checking only a tiny part of the proof. I had been working on this problem with several collaborators previously and published quite a few papers, but most of my mathematical work at that point was with Madhu Sudan, who was a professor at the MIT computer science department and who co-hosted me as a postdoc there (my other co-host was Professor Salil Vadhan at Harvard). Madhu and I agreed that efficient PCPs were intimately connected to the famous algorithm known as the Fast Fourier Transform (FFT), which solves a large, complex problem through recursive reduction, by breaking it into smaller and smaller pieces. FFTs let you zoom in and out of a structure quickly—like switching between close-up and wide-angle views of a very large puzzle.

One Friday morning, after many days spent with Madhu at the whiteboard and in coffee shops, I woke up, and a possibility presented itself. I say "presented itself" because that's what happened. I didn't sit by a paper pad or whiteboard; rather, I just saw it. That flash of insight was about recursion—breaking a big problem into smaller subproblems, just as the FFT does—and how this approach could lead to short, efficient proofs. I was elated, and both Madhu and I rejoiced.

By evening that same day, when everyone was busy with their weekend plans, I realized that my rejoicing was premature. I'd messed up and made a fundamental. I thought I'd broken down a single problem into two smaller but exact versions of itself, like taking a bunch of apples and splitting them in half, ending up with two batches of apples. But I had made a glaring error and ended up with the equivalent of one batch of apples and one of oranges—which obviously got me nowhere.

That weekend was brutal. Mathematicians know the feeling—your beautiful structure collapses, and you're left staring at the rubble. But the same stubborn curiosity that drives the original insight kicks in again. Madhu and I kept turning it over in our heads and eventually we saw a way through: Start the recursive process with a single batch that contains the exact same number of apples as oranges, and the recursion produces two smaller batches of half the size, each batch containing exactly half the number of apples and half the number of oranges. The flaw turned into a feature. We fixed it. The breakthrough came to be known as the *Ben-Sasson–Sudan PCP of Proximity* and paved the way for subsequent research.

So that's what breakthroughs look like from the inside. Not a single step from darkness to light, but a chain of advances, missteps, and recoveries. The emotional swing—from exhilaration to despair and back—is part of the process. Often the final insight is inseparable from the detour that nearly killed it. With this breakthrough, I picked up important life lessons along the way, and as a by-product, I hope I demonstrated determination and grit to my children.

The FRI Breakthrough

The second breakthrough I'd like to share came years later and was to me the most important, missing piece to making STARKs practical—the FRI protocol (short for Fast Reed-Solomon Interactive Oracle Proofs of Proximity, which I'll explain in detail later). At the time, circa 2016, Zcash and its ZK-SNARKs were already in production, and the world of cryptography was very content to keep using ZK-SNARKs for every use case. But I was not. I knew that a higher version of math could lead to better constructions. Rather, that was my gut feeling, but it wasn't yet supported by rigorous proof. You see, what we'd been coding in the lab was a system based on the PCP breakthrough with Madhu Sudan from 2003. It was the most efficient version of the PCP theorem known at the time. But it wasn't good enough.

The most important aspect of a validity proof is its "soundness error," which measures how likely a false statement is to slip through and be wrongly accepted. Think of it as the crack in the armor—a small vulnerability that an attacker might try to exploit. Validity proofs aren't airtight, and that's by design. To get their two magical properties—succinctness and privacy—we have to accept a small chance of error.

All cryptography involves some error probability. We reduce it by using long, unpredictable keys or passwords. But in 2016, the problem I faced was that the Ben-Sasson–Sudan PCP had too much error. Its recursive structure—splitting problems into smaller ones—came at a cost: Each split opened a new crack for attackers. After years of work, we still had what felt like a Galactic algorithm: mathematically sound, but only practical for problems too big to matter.

This really bothered me. All that effort into programming something and then realizing we'd made nearly no progress. It was this frustration, and thinking about concrete ways to attack the existing system, that led to the breakthrough. By dividing the main problem into subproblems in a slightly different way, and adding more randomness and more rounds of interaction between prover and verifier, we reached a groundbreaking result: the first protocol for proving the most central part of validity proofs (so-called "proximity testing") that had nearly optimal parameters (the best possible balance of practicality and security).

To explain: Proximity testing checks whether a given object (like a string of numbers) is close to something valid, without having to examine the whole thing. It's like checking whether a pool of water is clean by testing a few drops rather than the whole pool.

Before jumping in, here are a few terms that will help with what comes next: A *prover* creates a short proof that a computation was done correctly. A *verifier* checks that proof quickly, without redoing the full computation. The *soundness error* is the chance that a wrong answer slips through undetected. A *low-degree polynomial* is a kind of simple mathematical rule, like a smooth curve, and *proximity testing* checks whether some messy data is close to one of these simple rules, without checking every point.

Now, here's what happened.

We developed a protocol—known as FRI (short for Fast Reed-Solomon Interactive Oracle Proof of Proximity)—that hit a rare milestone: Both the prover and verifier ran as fast as mathematically possible. That alone is almost unheard of. Even better, the soundness error turned out to be much lower than expected.

I worked on FRI with three of my students—Iddo Bentov, Yinon Horesh, and Michael Riabzev—and it quickly became clear that this protocol would be a building block for the whole field. It solved the proximity testing problem with performance that couldn't be improved: The prover's time grew in direct proportion to the problem size, the verifier's time grew only slightly, and both were provably optimal.

At first, we could prove only modest soundness guarantees, though our instincts told us the underlying proof system was stronger. Over the next few years and a number of breakthroughs, working with Swastik Kopparty, Shubhangi Saraf, Dan Carmon, and Yuval Ishai, we tightened those proofs. The question that remains—closing the gap between what we see and what we can formally prove—is now tied to a $1 million prize from the Ethereum Foundation, a sign of how central this work has become to the future of blockchain.

Comparing the two breakthroughs, the second one didn't have quite the same Eureka feeling as the first. The tweaking came about more naturally and was obvious given the constraints and desire to improve soundness. Yet looking at the end result, it was clear to me that we'd achieved one of those fundamental results that would transform a field. And it has.

Ironically, though unsurprisingly, my fellow theoreticians disagreed. The paper describing the FRI protocol was rejected by several academic conferences. I did what all theoreticians do and submitted to "lesser" and "lesser" conferences, until ultimately it was accepted. The talk itself was attended by fewer than 10 listeners (some of them my own students who probably felt obliged to sit in). I was annoyed by the lack of recognition, but knew it didn't matter. Some results take a bit of time to sink in. Famously, the very first paper that introduced ZK proofs was rejected four times before being accepted on the fifth try. That didn't affect its importance; if anything, it heightened it.

Back to STARKs

Back to the paper announcing STARKs. Like the FRI publication, the STARK paper was widely rejected by academic journals—and for all the "right reasons." I say that tongue in cheek, riffing off a conversation I had back then with an academic friend—Gil Segev, a Professor of Cryptography from Hebrew University.

He quoted his advisor, Professor Moni Naor from the Weizmann Institute. Naor had said you'll know that there's a chance your work really matters if your paper gets rejected with all three of these reasons: Referee 1 says it's not correct, Referee 2 says it's not new, and Referee 3 says it's not interesting. (For context, in peer review, academic papers are evaluated by anonymous referees, often with wildly differing opinions.)

And so it happened that every round of peer review brought some mix of those three verdicts. It's impossible, said one. Another called it irrelevant. A third declared that the problem had already been solved. All of this criticism actually spurred us on.

We tightened the paper. We sent it to a committee that worked in this particular corner of crypto, and boom, it was accepted. A decade later, I went to a cryptography conference and gave a keynote about ZK-STARKs. After the talk, a researcher came up to me and said, "I was one of those who didn't believe this line of work makes sense. And I was wrong." It wasn't a grand apology; nobody needs that. It was simply a nod that the work had proven itself.

The Criticism

Even after the STARKs paper was published, I was still getting the sideways glances. Purist academics dismissed it as "just engineering"—packaging known math into a system, rather than actually proving a new theorem. Worse, it was engineering with no use case in sight. Protocol designers, security engineers, wallet and exchange builders, and others called it overcomplicated. They said there was already better cryptography in the form of ZK-SNARKs that did similar things, so why change?

Part of this criticism was cultural. I had started out as a theoretician, then moved toward making the ideas practical. So some theoreticians wondered why I was "wasting my time" on implementation. Meanwhile, many of those working in practical cryptography were already deeply invested in the standard mathematical tools for securing data, known as *elliptic-curve-based systems*. Elliptic curves are mathematical tools widely used in digital security. They allow for compact and fast cryptographic operations. Cryptographers working on elliptic-curve systems knew them inside out, had decades of constructions (cryptographic designs) built on them, and saw little reason to switch to something unfamiliar and more mathematically exotic.

(Mathematicians can be a critical bunch. They won't necessarily confront you in person. They'll simply snigger at your work behind your back. I saw this happen often enough: papers rejected without real engagement, talks politely ignored, dismissive comments passed quietly in corridors.)

I'd get feedback like "inefficient" or "irrelevant"—even though the numbers clearly said otherwise. It was easier for the reviewers to write the paper off than to relearn the math.

To many, STARKs seemed like tanks in a world of cavalry. Horses were proven, beloved, and well understood. Tanks were strange, complicated, and not to be trusted—yet. STARKs were powerful but unfamiliar—harder to operate and trust until proven in battle.

What STARKs Actually Do

Previously, we talked about how ZK-SNARKs worked and how their "trusted setup"—The Ceremony—was both ingenious and an Achilles' heel. STARKs resolved that paradox. They do away with the trusted setup entirely. They're transparent from the beginning, so anyone can verify them, and there's no secret key to hide, protect, or destroy.

STARKs also dispense with the elliptic curve cryptography that underpins ZK-SNARKs—a widely used technique in digital security that relies on these complex curves to encrypt data. This sounds abstract, but it's critical. Elliptic curve cryptography

(continued)

(continued)

is at risk from quantum computing—supercomputers that will make today's machines look feeble and that could "melt" existing security systems. STARKs use different cryptography that relies on simpler mathematical assumptions, which means they are secure even against that future threat. Cleaner assumptions; stronger guarantees. The "ZK" in ZK-STARKs stands for "zero knowledge," meaning the proof reveals nothing about the underlying data. This zero-knowledge property is what enables privacy. STARKs, like ZK-SNARKs, can be used in both public and privacy-preserving ways. They're not just secure; they can also be private.

Most importantly and surprisingly, setting up the verification never requires any process that's as expensive as checking the computation. STARKs offer true, succinct verification. That means the verifier can confirm that the result is correct without redoing the work. Recall that for an elliptic-curve-based ZK-SNARK, before the verifier can use them for the first time, it, or someone it trusts, must generate a "proving key" that is as long as the whole computation to be checked. With STARKs, this is never the case. The verifier, trusting no one, never needs to run a computation that's as long as what the prover is claiming. This matters a whole lot because it means that the size of computations checked with STARK technology easily scales with no limit in sight. With ZK-SNARKs, each one comes with an upper bound on the amount of computation that it can maximally guarantee.

Before we get into how STARKs work, let's recall the core scaling problem from earlier: On a blockchain, every node (every computer involved in securing the network) repeats every computation to make sure it's correct. This is what keeps the system trustless—but it's also why it slows to a crawl as usage grows. It's like requiring every commuter to check every other passenger's train ticket. ZK-STARKs take this a step further. Instead of making everyone repeat the entire computation, they let one party—the prover—do the work, and then publish a short mathematical proof that the work was done correctly. The prover does all the heavy lifting; others just need to glance.

This is where polynomials come in—mathematical expressions built from adding and multiplying numbers and variables in a fixed way, which can be used to represent the entire computation. ($2x$ and $5x^2$ are both examples of polynomials—simple mathematical rules involving powers of x.) A single polynomial is a formula that turns a sequence of inputs into a sequence of outputs by plugging each input into the variable x. ($2x^2$ turns the sequence (0,1,2,3) into (0,2,8,18).) And because of how math works, the outputs of a polynomial are tightly connected and display well-known patterns (for instance, all degree 2 polynomials, when plotted, look like parabola). This means you can check whether a sequence of numbers was derived using a fixed polynomial by an interactive process that chops the polynomial into smaller and smaller chunks and compares the chunks to one another. And the magic of it is that you don't read all the numbers of all these chunks—you can "spot check" a handful of them and be overwhelmingly sure the whole thing is correct. The process that does this is precisely the FRI protocol whose discovery I described above and is a central part of the way STARKs work. What STARKs do on top of FRI is to encode any computation as a series of polynomials, so that a proof is valid if all these different polynomials observe a certain mathematical pattern that can be checked by the verifier at random points. If the prover is lying, the chances of satisfying the mathematical pattern is vanishingly small.

Anyone can verify the proof quickly. Even if they don't trust the prover, they can trust the proof. The prover could be downright corrupt, think Darth Vader, or just inept, think Peppa Pig, but the design of the proof makes it impossible to slip in something false. If I've transferred $100 to someone, it's simply impossible for a bad actor to make it appear on-chain as $101 or $10,000.

From Theory to Infrastructure

In practice, STARKs make it possible to keep every computation completely honest while compressing vast workloads into a proof that can be verified exponentially faster than redoing the work. It's hard to adequately highlight the importance of this word, *exponentially*. It means not shaving minutes into seconds—but rather a leap so great that what once took years could shrink to moments—like the difference between walking and swimming from London to Sydney and taking a plane. It's not just efficiency; it's a new order of possibility. Refocusing on the blockchain aspect of it all, the heavy lifting happens off-chain, while the verification—lightweight and transparent—happens on-chain.

The implications are huge. STARKs resolve the seemingly unsolvable blockchain trilemma we encountered earlier: the idea that no system can be simultaneously scalable, secure, and decentralized. A quick reminder: The trilemma says you can have any two of the three, but not all—unless you use something fundamentally new. Until now, blockchain platforms had to pick two. With STARKs, you get all three.

At StarkWare, we've used STARKs to create countless proofs, each containing hundreds of thousands of transactions. Computation happens in the cloud, where it's fast and flexible. But everything is verified on-chain, where it's open and trustless. Each transaction takes only a fraction of the time and space on the blockchain. Space on the blockchain is like prime real estate—moving proofs off-chain reduces transaction costs by orders of magnitude, changing the economics completely. By slashing the cost per transaction and keeping verification transparent, STARKs make it possible to scale without compromising security or decentralization.

This isn't just theory. It's infrastructure—the foundation for the next generation of applications, from finance to identity to data storage and beyond. What will be different about them? The fact that they are run on a decentralized network means that the data you share and the funds you transact with will be truly owned by you, and only you, in the same way that you truly own a gold ring when you wear it on your finger.

Uri

The paper was out. The critics were circling. And the next step was obvious: If this cryptography was going to make a difference, it had to leave the page and enter the real world. That meant building a company around it—and it needed to be a "we," not an "I." I needed the right person to build it with.

Before there was funding—before there was even a name—there was Uri Kolodny. Serial entrepreneur, but in fields far from blockchain. We'd been friends for 30 years, our bond evolving from reckless university nights to dry dad jokes over family dinners. He's every founder's dream: someone who's seen you at your most foolish and still respects you. That kind of friendship comes with built-in honesty—the freedom to throw around ideas without fear of looking absurd.

When the STARK paper started to get attention, it occurred to me that Uri might be the right person to build with. But I wasn't sure—and neither was he. Even the strongest relationships can be strained by working together. We talked it through, got second and third opinions from other friends, and gave it the amber light.

Why not the green light? Uri is a man of great principle and blockchain sounded "scammy" to him. So I said, "Come to this conference I'm organizing at the Technion. Meet the people."

This was September 2017. I had been asked to organize the 2017 Cybersecurity conference on the topic of "blockchain" for the Technion's cybersecurity center in Haifa—usually held in a modest 150-seat room.

"Got anything bigger?" I asked university administrators.

"There's a 300-seater."

"Bigger?"

"Well, Churchill Hall has 600. Maybe 700 with standing room. But you won't need that."

"Anything bigger?"

They laughed. "You'll never fill even half of the Churchill auditorium."

"We'll see, but be ready to stop allowing registration."

I wasn't thinking about headcount; I was thinking about signal. So I started inviting friends:

- Vitalik Buterin—whom I mentioned earlier and who was, by then, the co-founder and public face of Ethereum, whom I first met over hummus at the Technion to explain ZK proofs to him, as a reporter for *Bitcoin Magazine*.
- Zooko Wilcox—fellow founder of Zcash alongside me, with whom I'd collaborated on privacy-preserving cryptography.
- Katie Haun—former federal prosecutor and rising crypto investor.
- Peter Van Valkenburgh—policy lead at Coin Center, one of the most thoughtful voices in crypto regulation.
- Arthur Breitman—mathematician and co-creator of the Tezos blockchain.

Every one of them said yes.

I kept asking the university if they wanted to cap registration. They kept waving me off. Two weeks out, signups passed 900. The university scrambled. On the day, the hall was packed, standing-room-only. The room pulsed with energy. It was peak ICO ("initial coin offering") season—noise everywhere—but the people in that room weren't chasing quick wins. They were shaping something real.

Uri saw it. Met the speakers, felt the current. And even though a few snake oil salesmen slipped in, he came away with his answer: He was in, full force. Uri served as StarkWare's first CEO from inception and through six years of rapid growth culminating with an $8 billion valuation, a story we'll tell in the next chapter. Uri left the position of CEO in February 2023 due to burning family health issues; he remains a close friend and serves on StarkWare's board to this day.

The Founding of StarkWare

When my co-author Nathan joined StarkWare in 2021, he asked to see our original pitch deck. I had to tell him it didn't exist.

The beginning of StarkWare was more wind than blueprint. The STARK paper had made the rounds, and those who saw what I saw—something foundational, not just clever—started to reach out. It was good timing. Crypto was in one of its upswings. Investors were looking for new ideas and new people to back.

We didn't have to knock on doors. People came to us. Friends, colleagues, strangers who'd read the paper and were moved to get in touch. Some of the best in the space. The message, again and again, was: "If you're doing this, I want in."

Startups often start life with a seed round of funding, priced on spreadsheets in a boardroom (pricing means determining the valuation of an early-stage startup). This one was a bit different. It was priced almost without words, in a rather pungent fish market in Shenzhen in the Chinese province of Guangdong. The genius co-founder of Ethereum, Vitalik Buterin, was at an academic crypto conference in the city, and so was I. We took a stroll together in the neighborhood and ended up at the market as the fishermen were closing their stalls for the day. Vitalik spoke Mandarin with the locals (apparently, one of the many languages he speaks). Then, at some point during our walk I asked: "Would you be willing to price our seed round?" He said "Err, hmm." In Vitalikese, this means "Yes, sure!" So I suggested a round of $6 million. Another "Err hmm," which meant "That's about right." And thus, the seed-round pricing was sealed, in a fish market in Shenzhen.

The funding round was oversubscribed before we'd even finished sketching what the company would be. What we had was conviction: Uri and I were absolutely certain about the tech, and the investors believed the timing was right. It felt less like a raise and more like a shared push—a group of people willing to help make something real.

The dream was now funded. All that remained was to build.

Mathematics Is Power

Some people want to start companies. Others write. Others teach. I've done a bit of all three. But the throughline, for me, is mathematics.

It hasn't always been easy. There were long stretches of confusion, of missing the point. But the pull was always there—the sense that math was pointing to something real.

The moments in my career that have meant the most actually didn't feel like I was inventing. Instead, they had the feeling of a discovery; of suddenly seeing something that was there all along, but you just didn't realize it until now; of unearthing something and dusting it down to discover a long-lost truth from a previous generation.

That's what STARKs felt like. We started with a concrete problem—how to make proofs scalable and private—and uncovered a structure that felt inevitable.

In a world of noise—headlines, posts, arguments—math offers something quieter: clarity. It doesn't depend on the speaker or the volume; it's just true.

Kids are told math is important, yet in many cases, they just don't see the point. "Why does it matter if my phone can do the calculation?" people ask. I get it. When we reduce math to workbooks in which kids perform boring sums and not much more, it's unsurprising. What they aren't getting to see is that math isn't really just about numbers. It's about structure and beauty. Just like music isn't about notes on a page; it's about experiencing the whole symphony. Math is really about seeing what holds. Noticing patterns. The math way of thinking changes how you approach problems—technical ones, yes, but also moral, social, even personal ones.

STARKs matter not because they're clever. They matter because they let you prove something without revealing everything behind it. They guard privacy without compromising truth. They don't demand trust—they build it. They enforce integrity on blockchains today and tomorrow, across the systems of nation-states. STARKs don't just protect privacy—they amplify integrity at scale.

That's math. That's what I still believe in. In a world that wobbles, it holds. And it soon pushed us from building an ecosystem to building a company to steward it.

CHAPTER 12

StarkWare: From Genesis to $8 Billion

There's a part of the StarkWare story you're about to hear that I absolutely believed would happen. That part is the recognition—by allies and competitors alike—of the importance and usefulness of STARKs. That was my hunch, my conviction, all along.

And there's a part that I never expected to tell: how I, as an academic, found myself at the helm of a company—StarkWare—worth $2 billion and that just six months later was valued at $8 billion.

The success of STARKs still feels improbable. A piece of pure mathematics, refined in obscure academic papers and debated in half-empty seminar rooms, somehow became the backbone of some of the most valuable infrastructure in crypto. We made a decision early on—and it wasn't the obvious one. Instead of guarding our intellectual property and keeping the core ideas locked away, we shared them freely. We built the infrastructure in public. And we invited others—including our fiercest competitors—to use the very same tools.

But what stands out just as much as the numbers and the tech success is the experience of building a company alongside a friend. Uri and I had already shared years of history when we decided to co-found StarkWare. Nothing tests a friendship like a startup—especially one growing at such a pace. We were lucky to have exceptional people in the mix from early on, including several people whom I'm grateful to see daily: Avihu Levy, Oren Katz, Gideon Kaempfer, and Lior Goldberg all joined within the first few months, and help me steer the company to this day.

Very early on, Uri gave me a stern talking-to. No more academic-style procrastination, he said. No more windsurfing when the northerly winds are calling. This was a company now—decisions had to be made, and quickly. He wasn't wrong. Though I'll admit, to this day there's still a sofa in my office, and I still "think things through" with my eyes closed. Occasionally—just occasionally—they remain closed for a brief power nap. And I still doodle with colored pencils in meetings just like I did in seminars.

The First Proof

Most of our early breakthroughs happened in a cramped coworking space, surrounded by the usual clutter—whiteboards full of sketches, cables everywhere. We would gather around someone's laptop, someone would say, "Wait, try that again," and then—something clicked. A piece of math that had lived only on paper suddenly ran. It worked. It did something nobody had seen before. There'd be a high five, maybe a grin, and then everyone got back to it.

But at some point, we knew we had to show the world. That happened in Prague, at a developer conference in 2018. It was standing room only. I was presenting alongside Avihu, whom I mentioned above—our first team member. Using nothing but the browser of an iPhone, Avihu generated a STARK proof, live on stage. No data center, no GPU farm—just unimaginable math running on a pocket-sized device. You could feel the crowd shift. Something abstract had just become real.

Math-to-Market Momentum

To make sense of what to build, Oren and Avihu did market research and then, right after the presentation in Prague, we convened around 25 crypto tech leaders—including the Paradigm and Pantera venture capitalists; the OGs ("Original Gangsters"), pioneering contributors from Ethereum and Bitcoin; and others. We discussed with them a number of possible projects that we might pursue.

The discussion was lively and interesting, and building a decentralized exchange (DEX) was under consideration. A DEX is a departure from the normal model for holding funds, in which an exchange looks after (or has custody of) your funds. The beauty of blockchain is that you can have the convenience of using an exchange, without the exchange ever controlling your money. In a DEX, trading remains in the hands of customers, never in the hands of the exchange.

Initially, it seemed Coinbase, the world's biggest Bitcoin exchange, would be our first customer for a DEX. Balaji Srinivasan, its CTO at the time, was blown away by the technology and offered to do a proof of concept (PoC) with us, which we did. And we passed with flying colors, only to be told the project would be shelved.

It wasn't about the tech. It worked. Everyone agreed on that. But what we hadn't realized was that our internal champion was on his way out. Balaji's excitement didn't have time to ripple outward. By the time it could've taken root, he'd moved on—and with him, the momentum. The silence that followed wasn't failure, exactly. It was the quiet that comes when a thread is dropped, and no one else picks it up.

Sometimes things don't stall because they're wrong. They stall because the right person left the room.

Years later, in 2022, the biggest crypto scandal to date unfolded as the FTX exchange collapsed and billions of dollars vanished. The implosion was made possible because, unlike DEXs, centralized exchanges (CEXs) that hold funds on your behalf were still the norm. CEXs operate through internal systems and the people running the exchange control customer funds. Hence the quips among crypto natives that whatever protections you take, there is no such thing as fully safe CEX.

FTX's founder Sam Bankman-Fried, once hailed as the industry's poster child, now stood at the center of the wreckage. I wonder, sometimes, if a name as huge as Coinbase had taken the superior DEX route, whether many family savings accounts might have been spared.

How STARKs Enforce Custody

With systems secured by ZK-STARKs, customers don't rely on dashboards or screenshots. They go straight to the immutable ledger—the authoritative blockchain—and see exactly what's in their wallet.

The key is custody. In these systems, assets never leave the user's control—not even for a moment. Even while interacting with a broader protocol, you retain full authority over your funds.

That's the critical difference. The exchange cannot move your assets. Only you can. And what enforces that isn't the goodwill of any operator—it's hard math.

The math of ZK-STARKs prevents the kind of deception that enabled FTX's collapse—because each customer maintains full custody of their funds all the time. The exchange cannot change your holdings. Only you can. And what enforces that integrity isn't the values of the operators. It's hard math.

In the end, the product that we built was not a DEX, but rather the infrastructure on which many, many DEXs, and other crypto apps run by others, could be built. It would be called StarkEx. We became the infrastructure folks, initially offering software-as-a-service and subsequently taking a different direction, which we will come to later in this chapter.

It's funny: Internally, we had been considering three different products, and the idea of StarkEx—a product for generating and bundling STARK proofs—was the one that excited us least. However, following the excitement in Prague, we changed paths, and soon enough we were bundling live blockchain transactions and generating proofs that could be posted to Ethereum. StarkEx, our first product and the first STARK system used in production, was live, and we weren't ready for the buzz it was about to create. To understand why, you don't need to know tech; you just need to know how any big city works. Let's use the ultimate example, New York.

What Was StarkEx Built to Deliver?

Think of a blockchain as Manhattan. It's prime real estate—expensive, congested, and limited. Every transaction takes up space, and when there's a surge in demand, costs go through the roof. For apps that need to handle a lot of activity—like games or exchanges—that can quickly make things unworkable.

But nobody builds a factory on Fifth Avenue. You shift operations to an industrial area where space is plentiful and it's easier to scale. That's exactly what StarkEx made possible: Do the heavy lifting off-chain; then send back a single STARK proof to the blockchain (Ethereum)—keeping all the security, without all the cost.

One of our early clients, Sorare, had been spending close to $1 million a week just to keep their football game running on Ethereum. The moment they switched to StarkEx, this $1 million a week on "gas fees" fell to almost zero—and suddenly, the game was accessible to a whole new group of players who'd previously been priced out.

StarkEx was the first proof of the utility and power of ZK-STARKs. Not in theory. Not in isolation. But in the wild. Quiet, precise, and transformational. It wasn't just a new product—it was the start of a new way of thinking about what blockchains could do.

The most compelling example of what StarkEx delivered is through its client relationship with dYdX, a DEX.

Before StarkEx, DEXs had a very hard time getting traction. They were throttled by the limited throughput that was possible on Ethereum and by the blockchain's high gas fees, making trading costly. Trading was not viable for the kind of small amounts that make daily use of an exchange attractive. At one point, transaction costs were so high for dYdX that it was forced to set a minimum trade size of several thousand dollars just to break even on transaction costs.

However, in September 2019, dYdX moved from Ethereum to StarkEx.

Almost overnight, dYdX's daily trading volume jumped from hundreds of thousands to billions of dollars. This feat was not just a first for StarkEx; it was a first for crypto. It was the first time ever that this model of doing the heavy lifting away from the main blockchain—taking it out of Manhattan—had been offered in the form of what we call today a Layer 2 (L2) network. This simply means a decentralized network that does this hard work before transactions hit the main blockchain, known as the Layer 1 (L1). StarkEx was the first instance of an L2 delivering mass-scale use of a decentralized exchange, putting DEXs in direct competition with CEXs. Today, there is a whole self-custodial Layer 2 economy, running on STARK-based networks and others, showing that scalable, trustless finance has moved from theory to reality.

Out in the Open

As we described above, one of the first—and most counterintuitive—decisions we made was to give the technology away. We didn't pursue any patents. No secrecy. No locked-down code. From the beginning, the core of STARKs was made public.

Practically, patents are rarely an effective way of protecting cryptographic infrastructure. It's different for drug companies—they must disclose their formulas and methods to a regulator. They can patent their formulas so others can't copy and profit from them for a fixed period of time. But in our world, there's no regulator demanding your algorithm before letting you ship your software. If someone wants to copy your code, a patent probably won't stop them. But more importantly, even if a brilliant intellectual property lawyer had offered us a watertight way to patent STARKs, we wouldn't have gone that route.

Because math isn't meant to be fenced off.

You don't patent a proof. You don't lock away the raw materials of knowledge. STARKs were born from open research, and we intended to keep them that way. This was no gesture of charity; it was a matter of principle.

In fact, we made not one but three counterintuitive "let's-share-our-stuff" decisions.

The first was what I've just described: no IP claims on STARKs themselves.

The second came shortly after we had turned the raw math into a working, pay-to-use platform. We could have imposed tight controls on it—limiting who could join, build, or use the platform. But we decided to go in the opposite direction because we envisioned something bigger—a public network that anyone could use to develop their own blockchain applications. That became Starknet. And today, Starknet is no longer governed by StarkWare. It's governed by a decentralized community. It's owned—like the internet—by nobody, and by everyone.

The third decision was to make the key building blocks of our system open source—publicly available for anyone to view, use, and build upon. Not just the easy parts, but the hard stuff too—the brain-twisting components that our engineers spent hundreds of hours perfecting. We shared much of it. Code that was once hidden deep inside StarkWare's infrastructure is now freely available for anyone to learn from, replicate, or adapt.

That's not the usual playbook in technology today. But blockchain culture is different, and StarkWare was never meant to be an ordinary company.

Letting Go and Boiling the Ocean

I often say—and I suspect people think it's a cliché or just corporate virtue-signaling—that the best part of running a company is admitting I've got it wrong. It happens when I'm against an idea and my colleagues present a counterargument with such clarity and substance that I change my mind.

The year was 2020, and members of the team started pushing for something I thought was a distraction: building our own programming language. I brushed it off. We had math. We had proofs. Surely we could adapt an existing language to fit our needs. Why reinvent the wheel?

But they kept at it. Lior, who I mentioned earlier, led the effort, alongside a talented engineer Shahar Papini, and my former PhD student and co-founder Michael Riabzev. Lior explained how a custom language would untangle the wiring between logic and proof—how it would make writing with STARKs feel natural, not like soldering wires onto a circuit board and hoping nothing would short.

To me, it still sounded like boiling the ocean. Programming languages are deeply entrenched. Developers argue passionately about whether to use Python, Rust, or C++. Getting adoption for a new one? Nearly impossible. And we weren't language designers—we were cryptographers.

But they made a compelling case. Every language is optimized for something. Python favors simplicity. C++ chases speed. CUDA squeezes everything out of GPUs to power games and simulations. If STARKs were going to scale, they deserved a language of their own.

Lior and the team built Cairo and carefully outlined its workings in a whitepaper[1] in order to meet those needs. Today it sits at the core of everything we do. It's clean, precise, and purpose-built. At first, Cairo was internal. But with the launch of Starknet, we opened it to the world—turning a bespoke tool into a universal gateway for anyone building with STARKs.

Cairo is to blockchain and zero-knowledge proofs what CUDA is to GPUs. CUDA, developed by NVIDIA, made it easy for developers to unlock the full power of graphics cards—not just for images, but for things like machine learning and scientific computing. It turned GPUs into general-purpose tools by hiding the complex hardware behind a clean programming model. Cairo does the same for STARKs. It lets developers write programs that can be proven efficiently, without needing to understand the underlying cryptography. What used to be hardwired and low-level becomes clean, fast, and programmable.

What I first saw as overreach has become foundational. Cairo didn't just make STARKs usable—it made them buildable. And like many good ideas, I had to be persuaded.

Investment and Valuation

In March 2021 we raised $75 million in our Series B round of funding. "Series B" normally means the third time a company raises money, usually after showing its idea works and is ready to grow (the first round is the "seed" round, followed by an A round, a B round, and so on).

It was a big moment for us, not just financially, but because we'd attracted funding from some serious players in the crypto world, and their vote of confidence meant everything to us.

The lead investor was Paradigm, a venture capital firm co-founded by Fred Ehrsam, who also co-founded Coinbase, and Matt Huang, a former partner at leading venture capitalist Sequoia. They'd built a reputation for backing category-defining crypto projects early on and helping them scale. Harvard, Yale, and Stanford had invested in their first fund.

The Series B didn't come with a public valuation, which sometimes happens for strategic reasons. But inside the blockchain community, it was still a big deal. It meant we had the backing not only of top-tier VCs, but of VCs who understood our technology and its potential.

Eight months later, in November 2021, we closed our Series C round. This time there was a public valuation: $2 billion. That was the first time anyone had put a public price tag on the company. And it made us a unicorn: that rare kind of startup that succeeds and acquires a valuation of more than a billion dollars.

The lead investor in the Series C round was Sequoia Capital, one of the most influential venture firms. They've backed Apple, Google, PayPal, WhatsApp, and Stripe. Having them as our lead investor was about more than just the capital. It was a signal to the broader market that scaling blockchain wasn't some fringe obsession—it was a mainstream technology play.

Outside of crypto, valuations like that can be hard to fathom. But to those inside our world—people who had been following our move from academic paper to real-world product—it made perfect sense. There was a lot of excitement. In blockchain circles, it felt like the gap between "people who know about us" and "people who should know about us" had just shrunk dramatically.

The Boost to $8 Billion

The ink was barely dry on the Series C paper and investors were clamoring for another funding opportunity.

Around six months later, in May 2022, we announced our Series D. It brought in $100 million and this time the company was valued at $8 billion. We'd grown in value by a billion dollars a month. That's staggering by any measure, all the more so because this was at a time when the wider crypto market was cooling. Prices were sliding. Sentiment was shaky. And yet, for us, investor demand was stronger than ever.

The round was led by Greenoaks Capital and Coatue, both major US tech investors, with participation from Tiger Global and existing backers—all with long track records of backing companies that went on to define their categories.

We carried on with our day-to-day business, while Forbes, Reuters, TechCrunch, CoinDesk, and other business and technology news sites ran headlines about our $8 billion valuation. The contrast between our humble, grounded culture and the media's extravagant expectations was almost comical. A few days later, the product team took a day off. No hotel suites, no champagne, no Lamborghinis— just a convoy of family cars pulling up beside a quiet river, coffee from the ice cream van, and then a senior team member, Tom Brand, grilled lunch for everyone in his garden. No fireworks. Just the same group of people, focused on building and getting the job done.

The endorsement of high-recognition investors was widely viewed as a vindication for our conviction that if blockchain could be made scalable, it could underpin the next era of the internet. We'd already shown that our technology could handle more transactions than Bitcoin—that we could slash costs, ease congestion, and still keep everything secured by Ethereum.

We built some of the most advanced infrastructure in crypto—not to win some startup race, but because we believed it was the best way to spend our lives. Whether StarkWare ends up the biggest name or not, we've already won in the ways that matter to us: by proving that math can change the world, and that integrity at scale is possible.

Launching Starknet

In late 2021, StarkWare worked on the launch of Starknet—a decentralized network where anyone, anywhere, could harness some of the most advanced mathematics ever used in production systems. At its core were STARKs, a cryptographic breakthrough that compresses massive computations into tiny, verifiable proofs.

For the first time, anyone could write code that leverages this "moon math" to build apps that scale globally—without any need at all to understand the deep math behind it. In a similar way that the internet democratized publishing and communication, Starknet democratized integrity, scale, and privacy—putting industrial-grade cryptography into the hands of any developer with an idea. They can now use ZK-STARKs to guarantee integrity—for any app or business case they choose.

This used to be the work of cryptography experts. StarkEx, for example, took serious math skills to build. But that's no longer the barrier. If you can write code, you can now build systems that prove every transaction was processed exactly as promised.

That's the magic of STARK proofs—the same engine that powered StarkEx now powers Starknet. They compress computations that might take hours into tiny mathematical receipts anyone can verify in milliseconds. Starknet uses these proofs just like StarkEx did:

by bundling thousands of transactions and posting a single proof to Ethereum. The shift is not in how it works, but in who can use it. What was once available only to partners is now open to all. Anyone can build on Starknet. Anyone can access that same scale and integrity without signing a contract or getting approval. The proving engine is the same. What's changed is who holds the keys.

Let me explain what this means in practice. You get a cryptographic stamp—proof that the system ran exactly as it should have. Nothing was skipped. Nothing was tampered with. Every line of code is executed properly, and you don't have to take anyone's word for it.

You could write a smart contract and let Darth Vader run it—and still sleep easy. He wouldn't be able to cheat or steal funds. The math won't let him.

We've taken the strongest tool we have for enforcing honesty—proofs—and made it available to anyone. It's like installing a fusion engine in your car. You don't need to understand nuclear physics. You just turn the key and go.

StarkEx was productive. High-performing. Beautiful in its own way. But closed. If you wanted in, you needed a contract with us.

Now think of Starknet like the internet. A digital space where anyone can build anything, without anyone's permission. But instead of building websites and regular apps, you can build blockchain-based apps—or as I like to wryly say, what we'll refer to in the future as "regular apps."

We took almost the entire tech stack we had created and threw open the gates for everyone to use it. What had previously been our walled garden had been transformed into a public space. Just like Shopify and Amazon have given every trader access to the type of platforms that were previously reserved for big businesses, Starknet put in the hands of everyone the power to build blockchain apps with global reach and scale to serve—if they take off— every citizen of the globe.

Cairo, the programming language we'd built for internal use, suddenly became usable by the public thanks to Starknet. Anyone could build applications harnessing Starknet's phenomenal capacity to bundle and compress huge numbers of transactions, without losing the security that made Ethereum trusted in the first place. Starknet was a DIY platform anyone could use, but the real change was much bigger than who was doing the building.

With StarkEx, we'd run the show—people who signed up were clients. With Starknet, there was no central operator. No one to approve or reject ideas. The network could head in directions we hadn't imagined, because it was shaped by everyone who used it.

We went from running a private service to creating public infrastructure. From tending a private estate to planting the first trees in a public park—a park where anyone could wander in, carve new paths, and make it their own. At the same time, we helped to establish the Starknet Foundation, an autonomous not-for-profit, to nurture, protect, and coordinate the Starknet network as a public good.

What Happened After Launch

Within days, people were building on Starknet. The network took on a life of its own. Soon enough, Starknet had its own culture, its own memes. In places I've never visited, and in languages I neither speak nor understand, there were meetups of developers and other interested parties. Everybody wanted to know about Starknet.

StarkEx had been about efficiency: doing the things you already wanted to do, but faster and cheaper. Starknet was different. It was a magnet that attracted people who wanted to build directly on blockchain without paying the usual heavy costs. And they started experimenting.

In some cases, Starknet was the perfect answer to an existing need. For financial applications, fast, low-cost transactions were a no-brainer. In other cases, it was a matter of pure exploration. For example, one developer built a physics engine that could run experiments on-chain, simply to see if it could be done.

If I look back on these months and ask what I found the most energizing, it was the growing realization in the blockchain community that scaling in general, and Starknet in particular, is not just about making the old things cheaper. It is about making new things possible.

Let me unpack that. Each and every time you interact directly with Ethereum, you pay—and it's expensive. That's why so many ideas never get off the ground. Many unrealized ideas are fun, useful, or ingenious, but the transaction fees are prohibitive.

Take gaming. You'd never design a computer game where every move costs you real money to record on-chain. It would be like playing Monopoly and paying real money each time you build a house. It just wouldn't make sense. But with Starknet's scalability, that calculation changes. Suddenly, you can do things so cheaply and quickly that your imagination starts to go somewhere else entirely.

Imagine if flying abroad suddenly cost the same as a local bus trip—and magically got you there at the same time. You'd broaden your horizons. Why go for a day out at your local park when you could fly off to another continent? Why eat pizza at the Italian restaurant on your street corner when you could just as easily jet off to Rome? You'd go shopping in New York, Milan, Dubai, Hong Kong, wherever you fancied. It would transform the way you think about where you can go and what's possible.

That's the shift Starknet is driving now—a world of new possibilities that were previously unthinkable. Some people are playing with the technology for the sheer joy of it; others are building what they believe could be the apps of the future.

It's Blockchain On Speed

Would you like to run the equivalent of Nasdaq for a day? A bank? What about an auction house for collectibles? This idea—which might sound crazy—is already a reality on Starknet.

And when I say that, I don't mean a crazy person telling the world to trust his or her "Nasdaq." I mean any person being able to set up such a venture that has a cryptographic stamp proving that he or she is carrying out all computation correctly.

You might remember the mailroom analogy from the introduction—the one in which a device scans all the credit card bills in the company's mailroom and is able to verify that every line of computation, adding up, has been carried out correctly? Well, Starknet is like taking that scanning device out of the credit card company's print room and putting it on your desk at home. It's hardwired to follow strict cryptographic rules—rules you can't bend or bypass. You run your computation locally. When you're done, the device produces a cryptographic stamp of approval, certifying that everything was done by the book. That stamp is powerful enough to write the result directly to the blockchain. The chain doesn't replay the steps—it just checks the certificate and moves on.

Let me break down what Starknet is facilitating and how.

Economies run on parallel rails. It would be absurd if they didn't. You'd need to wait for the burger joint to finish using the system to get your payment processed before you could invest in the S&P. Thousands of markets function simultaneously, and moment by moment, countless public records are updated. This is actually part of the reason stock trades don't settle instantly: untangling who did what, where, and when across many systems takes time.

Blockchains—including Bitcoin, Ethereum, Zcash, and many others—don't work like this. All transactions must stand in the same line. It's basically building an infuriating bottleneck into the design, through which every transaction must pass. Every trade, game move, and contract runs in sequence, verified and recorded by the chain one step at a time.

If that doesn't sound bothersome, it's like asking you to give up your computer that can do numerous things simultaneously (you just need to see how many apps I have running at once) and instead agree to use an old PC that had a one-track mind and could only handle one task at once. With such a computer, switching tasks meant quitting one program to open another. Would you agree to such a switch? Clearly not—you want multithreading, as we call it.

In economic terms, it's just how the world works: multiple transactions, activities, and markets unfolding in parallel, across time zones and systems.

It was clear to all of us involved in developing Starknet that it should bring multithreaded logic to blockchain. After all, STARK proofs lend themselves to this setup. With STARKs, the chain doesn't need to be executing every transaction. Rather, any user, developer, or group can process a large batch of transactions off-chain. They send a single cryptographic proof that says: I did the math, I followed the rules, and here's the result.

So what is Starknet, the chain, doing? It's checking just that proof. The entire batch is accepted in one move. It's like handing a cashier one trusted receipt instead of scanning each item in your cart.

What makes all of this possible? The way that Starknet is built—from the ground up to trust these cryptographic proofs. Other blockchains don't have the architecture or math to accept a result without redoing the work themselves.

What do we gain from this? Three big things:

Scale: Diverse applications running at once, without clogging the same pipeline.

Speed: Very fast updates to the blockchain because the chain checks just the proof, not every transaction.

Openness: Anyone can build whatever they like. It could be a market, game, or community economy—without permission, credentials, or massive infrastructure.

Privacy—Only the operator sees the transactions; everything else can be shielded, offering a smooth user experience with strong privacy.

Opportunity—This is the most exciting part. A multi-threaded blockchain is entirely new, and entrepreneurs will use it to build everything from niche auction houses to vibrant marketplaces—closer in spirit to the real-world bazaars we love. It opens the door to countless applications driven by local, small-scale creativity.

When we say a "multi-threaded" blockchain economy, this is what we mean. It's not just more efficient—but actually more expressive. Different activities—short or long, serious or silly—can unfold simultaneously, each verified independently, and then all settled together.

Starknet applies decentralization not just to participation, but to the very act of creating blocks. It pushes control to the edges, giving anyone the tools to run a system of their own.

Back to Bitcoin

What's exciting today isn't just the *what* of our work; it's the *where*. Starknet began as a scaling solution for Ethereum. The idea was to make things faster, cheaper, and more scalable—and it did just that. But having shown what's possible there, we're now applying the same approach to an even bigger challenge: expanding the Bitcoin economy.

In the Bitcoin white paper, Satoshi explains he's creating it to "allow any two willing parties to transact directly with each other without the need for a trusted third party."[2] This ability to transact directly means something far greater than what Bitcoin affords us today. Bitcoin needs to not just find a way to scale, but also a way to allow people to transact in any way they want, which includes investing, lending, borrowing, and creating shared enterprises.

The way Satoshi saw this broader Bitcoin economy developing was by allowing Bitcoin to interface and integrate with separate chains that do not clog Bitcoin but still settle onto it.

But today, more than 99% of Bitcoin is just "hodled" (people don't trade their Bitcoin—they hold on to it; the crypto community turned a famous 2013 typo when someone wrote, "I'm hodling," into its proud slang). It's an anomaly that so little of the best-performing asset of the past decade is unproductive. If you had a financial asset, wouldn't you like it to generate yield in some way, to use it as a way to transact and conduct business in the world?

That's precisely what we're now doing on Starknet. Our mission is simple: Scale the Bitcoin economy; grow Bitcoin GDP. Allow people to borrow against their Bitcoin; to invest what they borrow; and to create, fund, and support new Bitcoin businesses that will disrupt and replace the centralized financial world as we know it.

Building Starknet to scale the Bitcoin economy is a bold move. And for me, it's actually also a thrilling full-circle moment. This whole story began at the Bitcoin conference in 2013 (described in detail earlier in the book). Now, years later, we're building infrastructure that could help Bitcoin evolve from a static store of value into something used daily by millions.

The test is as simple as it is ambitious. Can Bitcoin pass the toothbrush test? By which I mean, can you use it twice or more per day, without thinking about it? That's what we're working on: developing the tech and building the financial layer to make it real.

In essence, we're building Bitcoin's everyday-use layer. And my colleagues and I share a feeling that it's the most exciting challenge of our lives so far.

To understand the significance of all this, let me tell you how I recruit.

We need the very best engineers. But most of them have no real interest in blockchain. They see code, not concepts. And it may surprise you, but even for an $8 billion company, convincing top engineers to join still takes work.

So here's what I tell them.

It's a three-part pitch I've been using since 2018, when we were just getting started. And honestly, I still use the same version today.

First: I believe, completely, that ZK-STARKs, the math behind everything we do, will shape the future. Not just of blockchain, but of the internet itself. One day, these systems will be as foundational as TCP/IP. You won't notice them. They'll just be there, running underneath.

Second: like any early mover, we might not be the ones who make the most money from this tech. Others may build on it. Some might even commercialize it better than we do. I don't think that'll happen, yet I've seen enough history to know it could. Being first doesn't always mean ending up on top.

Third, if you're smart and curious, you should be thinking hard about how you spend your time. Not your money, not your title—just your time and attention. That's the real currency. And there's something deeply satisfying about using it to build systems that enforce honesty. Where math becomes a check on power. That's not hype. That's the actual work.

That's what I offer people when they ask why they should join us. No big sell. Just clarity on what we're building, and why it's worth a chunk of your life.

CHAPTER 13

The Harshest Critique: Do We Even Need Crypto?

Critics raise many objections to crypto: among them scams, hacks, and regulatory ambiguity. But one criticism is more fundamental, more sweeping, and potentially more damaging than any other. Because this book is about a broad, big vision, I'm going to focus on the harshest criticism: the claim that crypto is simply unnecessary.

The Argument Against Crypto

I work in a profession of meddler-economists and technologists who keep trying to fix things even when critics say, "If it ain't broke, don't fix it." Crypto is a hammer in search of a nail, a solution looking for a problem. It disrupts without diagnosing, arriving ahead of its justification.

And worse than being unnecessary, crypto is—according to this critique—more harmful than the institutions it seeks to replace.

Don't dismiss this critique out of hand. It's not the argument of dinosaurs. It comes from some of the most respected minds in economics and finance. Chief among them: Paul Krugman, Nobel Prize–winning economist, research professor at the City University of New York's Graduate Center, and longtime columnist for *The New York Times*. He is one of the most widely read and cited economists alive, known for his ability to explain complex ideas with clarity.

He has called Bitcoin a "cult."[1] He's described crypto as "technobabble"[2] and compared it more than once to a Ponzi scheme.[3] His central argument: Crypto doesn't do anything useful that existing systems don't already do better. And far from helping, crypto introduces new risks and inefficiencies without delivering commensurate benefits. To Krugman, this isn't just a bad investment—it's a regression. A distraction. A potential disaster.

What's most interesting is his core premise: that humans are already wired to reward trustworthiness. We don't need technology to do it for us.

At the heart of Krugman's critique is a worry that prioritizing code-based trust over human judgment devalues the social systems we've built. Reputation, he argues, is what compels institutions—banks, card networks, payment platforms—to behave responsibly. Because they don't just want your trust today; they want it tomorrow too.

His view is that finance already works fine without cryptographic guarantees, thanks to the logic of repeated interactions. Banks treat you fairly today so that you don't leave them for another bank. In that framing, crypto's "trustless" systems aren't just misguided—they're dangerous. They discard a system built on credibility and replace it with one that lacks oversight, accountability, and a proven track record.

The Counterargument

Krugman's view is consistent, coherent, and grounded in mainstream economics. But it misses something. Because we're not living in a world that looks the way it always has. Today's heavily intermediated, third-party financial system is an anomaly.

Across human history, most commerce was peer-to-peer and face-to-face. Even when banks took hold in the seventeenth century, they acted mainly as vaults for safekeeping and as lenders. Until the arrival of computers and internet commerce, transactions were still largely direct. Even checks were often passed around between people without being formally redeemed at a bank.

What we have now—a system in which even the smallest payments must pass through centralized institutions—is historically unusual. My son's class events, for instance, often involve digital contributions routed through group messages and apps. What used to be a piggybank or cardboard box passed around is now a web of third parties.

Blockchain may run on modern tech, but its underlying values are ancient.

For millennia, people transacted directly—goods for goods, labor for shelter, favors for food. Trust was social, not institutional. You didn't need a bank to vouch for a deal; you looked someone in the eye. Ownership didn't require a digital ledger; you held the item in your hand. Reputation mattered, but it was personal, local, and human scale.

Contrast that with today, where we rely on banks for everything. Paychecks, bills, rent—most of us can't opt out, even if we're unhappy. Often we don't choose the best option from a vibrant market—we settle for the least bad and hope nothing changes overnight. When things go wrong, you don't get answers. You get "hold" music.

And reputation is not serving us well. We are all dedicated users of central services that start off helpful and slowly decay into rent-seeking intermediaries. This pattern of platform decay has become such a phenomenon that journalist Cory Doctorow gave it a name that has stuck: "enshittification."[4] What he means is that platforms lure us in with utility and openness. Then they tighten the screws—more ads, more restrictions, more ways to be locked in. Benefits flow upward, but risks stay with the user.

What's odd is that we seem to accept it in the very place we should be most cautious: our systems of money, coordination, and trust.

In almost every other sphere, we know that markets tend to outperform central planning. We recognize that we have better outcomes when there is competition and openness, not gatekeeping. But in finance and trust infrastructure—the digital plumbing of modern life—we've traveled in the opposite direction: more centralization, fewer opportunities to exit, and less choice.

Blockchain is a redesign: a way to build infrastructure that resists "enshittification" at the root, because no one actor controls the rules.

Yes, centralized systems often work—until they don't. When they break, the impact is enormous.

From Cyprus to Argentina, people have seen their savings frozen or erased by top-down decisions. Even in the United States, accounts can be frozen, access revoked, or decisions made by invisible algorithms.

Centralized systems may be efficient most of the time, but so are dictatorships. Live under one, and you quickly learn the price of efficiency without recourse.

Not all breakdowns are political. Some are just bugs. In 2025, a routine configuration error at Cloudflare—a company that quietly routes a vast share of global internet traffic—brought down hundreds of thousands of websites. It wasn't malicious. But that's the point: even well-run, well-intentioned centralized systems can become silent single points of failure. Their very convenience hides their fragility.

Blockchain offers something else: not just efficiency, but accountability. Not just promises, but proofs. And an alternative to the consolidation of centralized power that had millions hopelessly clicking "refresh" on that day in 2025, wanting to scream.

Blockchain doesn't introduce fragility. It corrects it. It doesn't replace trust. It retools it for the digital world, where more and more of life now unfolds. And it does so in a way that's equitable, transparent, and—at its heart—democratic. Democracy is slow and often messy, but it's fairer than any alternative.

Ask yourself which of the two models sounds more fair to you? Which one resonates better with the principles of free society? On the one hand we have Bitcoin and blockchain that operate under the three novel principles we previously described: (1) everyone-is-invited to operate the system (anyone can participate in running and securing it), (2) radical transparency (the rules and transactions are publicly visible) and (3) incentivized integrity (honest participation is rewarded, and those operating the system fairly share its proceeds).

And on the other hand we have the model running finance over the past few decades in which central parties like banks and payment processors mediate each and every transaction we wish to do. Contrasted with the three principles of Bitcoin, banks operate under three diametrically opposite principles: (1) leave-it-to-the-bank (only approved institutions get to operate the system), as opposed to everyone-is-invited, (2) radical opacity (operations and decision-making are largely hidden from public view) as opposed to radical transparency, and (3) spoils-go-to-few (profits accrue to a small group rather than being broadly shared) as opposed to incentivized integrity and fair sharing of profits. This last principle of spoils-go-to-few is by now, with the rise of banking behemoths, combined with the too-big-to-fail principle (institutions so large that governments feel compelled to rescue them), which translated spectacularly in the aftermath of the 2008 crash to "banks screw up, public bails them out, bankers keep their huge bonuses."

Many imagine the current system as timeless. But that's a fiction. The world of intermediated, surveilled, highly centralized commerce is a recent development. My father, not long ago, could give money to his brother directly. Most purchases were cash in hand. That freedom is rare now. Near-hourly, we depend on institutions we didn't choose—and can't meaningfully exit.

Blockchain isn't rebellion. It's a return to something older, but newly possible at scale: direct, transparent, community-enforced exchange. It is a counterweight to a world where every action is routed, filtered, and monetized.

We can now imagine possibilities that were once out of reach. Especially for those who lived through 2008, the financial crash that brought crypto into focus, it's clear the old systems are strained.

Blockchain isn't perfect. But it is necessary. Not frictionless—just essential, given the path we're on. Not because the old ways have no merit, but because they've hit their limits. The future of trust won't be about nostalgia. It will be about redesign.

We can't undo the digitization of life. But we can decide how to live within it—on whose terms, with what safeguards, and with which tools.

I live in a country with decent banking. I've built a company, raised funds, and have a global voice and platform—indeed, I have written this book. But most people who suffer under the current financial system don't get heard. Their needs are underrepresented. So yes, many think of crypto and blockchain as a boon to the privileged—but the truth is that for those without privilege, it may become indispensable.

That's why I see crypto and blockchain infrastructure not just as a technical opportunity, but as a moral one. If we have the resources to build infrastructure that can serve all of humanity, it's our job not to limit ourselves to what already works for the few.

The real question isn't: "Do we need blockchain?" It's: "How long can we afford not to?"

CHAPTER 14

Stablecoins and Meme Coins

So far, we've explored how blockchain technology can serve as the foundation for new forms of shared infrastructure and for systems that secure identity, enforce digital rules, and record data, and do all of this in a tamper-proof way.

We have discussed how money is just one kind of record, and how documents are also records, and can and should also be anchored to blockchains. Identity, contracts and much more. But when records live inside separate institutions, power follows whoever controls the database. What blockchains introduce is a shared layer of integrity beneath all of this.

That can still sound abstract. So to show how this story is already unfolding in practice, this chapter turns to concrete examples of the infrastructure blockchain enables today. This is not the end point of the technology—but it is an early, revealing wave of real use.

One of the clearest and most widely adopted answers is the *stablecoin*, a digital token engineered to hold a stable value, usually pegged to the US dollar. And while that may sound mundane, stablecoins are arguably the most successful blockchain-based product to date. Millions use stablecoins such as USDT (Tether) and USDC (USD Coin) to send payments and store digital dollars. Together, these tokens (and other stablecoins) move billions of dollars daily across blockchains, quietly reshaping how value can (and does) move across the internet.

Let's unpack what a stablecoin is, how it works, and why it matters, especially if you live in a place where traditional finance (TradFi) systems are expensive, unreliable, or slow.

The Stablecoin

As we've noted, a stablecoin is a digital asset designed to hold a stable value—typically by being pegged one-to-one to a fiat currency like the US dollar. Think of it as a blockchain-based version of a dollar: transferable 24/7, programmable, and reliably worth a dollar. As of mid-2025, there were around 170 such tokens in circulation.

Here's how it works. You give an issuer a dollar, and they mint a stablecoin—a digital token with the value of a dollar—and send it to you via a blockchain transaction. You can then send that token to anyone, anywhere, at any time. And when you're ready, you can redeem any such token in your possession for the original dollar: you send it back to the issuer, the digital token is destroyed, and the original dollar lands back in your bank account. If hearing that it's "destroyed" sounds jarring, just think of it like an IOU note that you may write a friend that is ripped up once the debt is settled.

In that sense, it's not actually brand new. It's actually the way that paper money originally worked. You went to a trusted goldsmith with gold, and the goldsmith issued a handwritten note promising to redeem it for the same amount of gold. The time came when people stopped redeeming the notes and just traded the paper, as there was enough trust in society that they would be honored. Stablecoins use the same principle in the digital era. You deposit dollars, but not to a goldsmith—to a stablecoin company. It gives you a token that anyone else can accept or redeem. What has changed is the speed, reach, and transparency of the system that makes it possible.

That scenario may not sound revolutionary. But it is—especially if you live in an emerging market or need to move money across borders, or if you don't want to deal with the delays, fees, and restrictions that come with traditional finance, including, for a relatable everyday example, a transaction being declined by your credit card company.

I recently spoke to an attorney who was traveling across Brazil and the United States and was trying to buy a wedding gift from a UK department store. The attorney understood finance, but the cross-border transaction turned into a multiday frustration. Standard systems simply didn't work. The contrast was stark—and revealing. A problem that stumped credit cards and bank networks was solved, in seconds, by a dollar-backed token and a smartphone. They simply used their debit card to buy $100 worth of USDC (United States Dollar Coin), a popular stablecoin, on Coinbase, a cryptocurrency exchange and platform. Then they copied the QR code provided by the department store's crypto checkout page and hit Send. The token landed in the store's wallet in roughly 30 seconds and cost a few cents in fees. Traditional payment networks—or *legacy rails*—couldn't manage what a blockchain-based token handled effortlessly.

Stablecoins work because they strip out the intermediary. No banks, no currency conversion delays, no unclear fees. Just value moving, securely and almost instantly, from one wallet to another, thanks to the finality of blockchains, which takes seconds, not days, and confirms your true ownership.

Let's step away from blockchain, just for a moment, to appreciate the problem it is often trying to solve: moving money easily and reliably.

In 2016, a nonprofit backed by India's major banks launched the Unified Payments Interface (UPI), a real-time system that lets users send money instantly between bank accounts. All someone needs is a UPI ID—no cards, no intermediaries. UPI spread rapidly, including in rural areas, because it met a real need with an elegant solution.

Stablecoins, when built on public blockchains, offer something structurally different. They don't aim to replace UPI; they aim to extend the same promise to a broader context that's global, permissionless, and programmable. That's the key distinction: UPI is domestic infrastructure built for a single country. Stablecoins, by contrast, run on borderless blockchains—they're designed from the start for global use.

Even in countries with strong domestic systems like UPI, many people already work (or want to work) for clients abroad. So the need isn't just fast payments, but fast cross-border payments, without the delays, fees, or friction of TradFi. Stablecoins aren't here to compete with UPI since they fill in what UPI can't yet do well: enable cross-border settlement, support open innovation, and serve as money that can be integrated directly into software—not just sent through it.

For billions of people, especially in regions with unstable currencies or limited financial infrastructure, reliable payments aren't a gimmick; they're a breakthrough. The fact that stablecoins can move money across borders, cheaply and reliably, is what makes them especially compelling. Even in rich countries, many people are locked out of bank access, whether that's due to missing documentation, a closed account, or bankruptcy. They can't use the slick fintech apps, but they can hold a dollar stablecoin and pay peer-to-peer (P2P) via their smartphone.

If you've ever tried sending a few hundred dollars abroad with a wire or Western Union, you'll know the drill: lines, forms, fees, and overall, a process that's anything but instant. Compare that to a stablecoin transfer that's wallet to wallet (typically taking just minutes) and the difference becomes obvious.

Among a crowd of highly volatile cryptocurrencies, stablecoins stand out. Their value is typically pegged to fiat currencies, like the US dollar, making them both stable and convenient. With those key attributes, they are quietly chipping away at the age-old notion that only banks can move money.

The Meme Coin

If the stablecoin is the sensible parent, then another type of crypto, the meme coin, is the wild child. Both reflect a broader curiosity, sometimes ideological, often opportunistic, about alternatives to traditional money. But the meme coin isn't pegged to anything and isn't backed by any reserves. Its value is determined by viral trends, hype, celebrity endorsements, and investor speculation.

You've probably heard of the most famous of meme coins—Dogecoin. It was created in 2013 as a parody of crypto hype. In an ode to internet randomness, it featured the face of a Shiba Inu dog from a then-popular meme. The name itself—Doge—was a misspelled, deliberately absurd take on "dog," meant to mimic a certain meme-speak aesthetic. And the coin had no serious technical innovation behind it. That was the point.

Oddly, what began as satire gained a following, then a market cap in the billions. Dogecoin became a kind of cultural currency. It resonated as a way to tip creators online, sponsor NASCAR racing drivers, and—perhaps most famously—ride the wave of attention from Elon Musk, the world's most followed tech magnate, who repeatedly tweeted about it.

Musk's involvement wasn't just noise. His jokes and casual endorsements moved markets. At one point, Dogecoin's value surged more than 500% in a single week. It was the first time a cryptocurrency born from a meme had prompted serious scrutiny from US financial regulators.

Both stablecoins and meme coins reflect a broader curiosity—sometimes ideological, often playful—about alternatives to traditional money. But where stablecoins aim for reliability, meme coins chase attention. They're built for spectacle, not stability. The act of creating a currency on a whim is itself part of the message—a quiet mockery of the gatekeeping in traditional finance. In the same way Maurizio Cattelan's Comedian (2019)—a banana duct-taped to a wall that sold for $120,000 and later became a $6.2 million art-world spectacle—mischievously questioned what counts as "art," meme coins ask, just as provocatively: what counts as money?

You might be thinking Bitcoin isn't pegged to anything either, so what's the difference? The value of a meme coin is purely viral speculation. Bitcoin derives its worth and its increasing popularity from its decentralized, secure network. There are strict controls on how new Bitcoins are created and released into circulation. People treat it as a kind of digital gold, so its price reflects scarcity, trust, and utility—not just hype. You may ridicule this, but meme coins are a compressed digital form of fashion. Every year shirts and socks could surge in price tenfold and a hundredfold if they have the right logo and brand imprinted on them, and their main value is memetic. You may love fashion or hate it, but you have to acknowledge it represents a sustainable human desire—to look good. Meme coins are a bit like that.

Meme coins offer no stability, no guarantees, and have no official blessing. And that's exactly the point. They're not a hedge against inflation—they're a fashion item modeled like a middle finger to the system. A reminder that money, too, can be a kind of performance. One that doesn't need to play by anyone's rules.

So if stablecoins are the responsible adult in the room—calm, consistent, but quietly disruptive—meme coins are the unruly teenager. They don't want to be safe. They want to be free.

Both, in their own way, reflect a shift in how we think about money. One is practical, the other playful. But each shows that money is no longer solely what governments say it is. It's what people choose to trust—and what systems they choose to use.

Remittances

If stablecoins have sometimes seemed like that hammer without a nail—a solution in search of a use case—remittances are the counterpoint: a pressing, clear need meeting a viable tool.

Every year, migrant workers around the world send more than $600 billion home to their families. These payments, or *remittances*, are lifelines—not just transfers of money, but of opportunity, security, and dignity. They cover rent, food, school fees, and medicine. And yet the global infrastructure for moving this money is still inefficient and expensive. According to the World Bank, the average cost of sending remittances remains more than 6%. That means for every dollar sent, recipients often get just 94 cents. The reason for this is that the global financial system is not one unified network (like a blockchain) and has no single ledger of trust. Agreeing on such a ledger would be impossible from a geopolitical point of view—who controls it? The United States? The G7? Because there is no single global ledger or governance, the system is fragmented, and paying across borders is slow, costly, and labor-intensive.

In this context, the rise of stablecoins offers something genuinely useful. A recent study by Lennart Ante, published in the academic journal *Telematics and Informatics*,[1] provides one of the most comprehensive looks yet at how and why people are turning to blockchain-based alternatives. Ante surveyed 866 US-based adults who regularly send money abroad. More than a quarter—26%—had already used stablecoins for some transactions.

The appeal isn't hard to understand. Stablecoins like USDT (United States Dollar Tether) and USDC (United States Dollar Coin) are live on decentralized networks that span the globe, like the internet. That means they can move across borders instantly, often at a fraction of the cost of traditional services. In some cases, fees drop to 1–2%, typically covering blockchain network costs and platform service fees. Even though the system is decentralized, users still pay small fees to the networks that process transactions, in some cases, to exchanges or wallet providers that offer added convenience. And unlike bank wires or money transfer services, they're not constrained by business hours, paperwork, or physical branches. All that's needed is a smartphone and an internet connection.

Ante's study also explores who is using these tools—and why. Adoption is higher among younger, more educated users, and particularly among those making higher-value transfers. But more revealing is what drives continued use. Those who try stablecoins and find them useful tend to keep using them. The reasons aren't ideological. They're practical. It works. It's fast. And it saves money. That said, paying for everyday necessities, such as groceries, gas, and your mortgage, with stablecoins is still fairly niche. Only a handful of online merchants, select national payment apps, and a few crypto-friendly local businesses accept them directly. In most cases, you'd have to cash out back into a local currency via an exchange or P2P app.

Skills That Drive Stablecoin Adoption

Ante's study showed that digital and financial literacy feed one another. Those who can navigate online tools—like choosing a stablecoin, managing a wallet, and understanding how to move money in and out of crypto—are far more likely to adopt stablecoins. As people gain hands-on experience and familiarity with these mechanics, trust will build and, in turn, make further use easier and more likely in the future. Ante refers to this as a "virtuous cycle"—the opposite of the confusion and opacity that characterizes much of the legacy remittance system.

Hurdles remain: reliable internet access and cheap data; easy on-/off-ramps; exchange access in more countries; clear, consistent rules; simple wallet user experience (UX) and recovery; compliant KYC/ID for the unbanked; and consumer protections against scams. Adoption will remain uneven until these improve, but the momentum is real.

What's striking is how unassuming this shift has been. Stablecoins don't make headlines for double-digit gains or massive collapses. But quietly, in wallets and communities around the world, they're beginning to displace one of the most entrenched forms of financial intermediary.

Stablecoins are also a good example of how the blockchain story is evolving in an unexpected and important way—not just technically, but geopolitically. A few years ago, it was easy to predict that the relationship between Washington and crypto would be largely adversarial. One represented regulation, the other decentralization. Crypto was about exit; the state was about control. That binary still shows up in headlines and hearings. But behind the scenes, something more interesting is taking shape.

The GENIUS Act

Stablecoins are reframing the conversation precisely because they peg themselves to traditional currencies—they've taken what looked like a clash of systems and turned it into a potential convergence. In the United States, they've made key institutions ask not, "How do we stop crypto from undermining the dollar?" but rather, "Can crypto help the dollar stay relevant?"

That shift came into sharp focus with the passage of the GENIUS Act—the "Guaranteed Electronic Nationwide Infrastructure for Ubiquitous Stablecoins" Act in July 2025. The name might be a mouthful, but the law was real. Backed by the US Treasury and passed with bipartisan support, it marked a significant turning point. Its passage with bipartisan support reflected a shared recognition across the aisle: preserving the dollar's global relevance in a digital age requires embracing, not resisting, innovation.

On paper, the GENIUS Act laid out a regulatory framework for stablecoins. But in substance, it did something more profound: It formalized what had been industry practice—backing stablecoins 1:1 with short-term US government assets—and enshrined it in law. It also redirected who benefits from that backing: Where the yield had flowed to companies like Circle and Tether that aren't banks but that issue stablecoins, the Act steered stablecoin reserves into bank-run structures and T-bill holdings—short-term US government debt seen as safe and liquid—pulling payment interest income ("float") back onto bank balance sheets.

That second effect—diverting interest from private issuers to banks and the US Treasury—matters to Washington. It means more of the growing stablecoin reserve pool is now funding public debt instead of private profit. Banks already earn interest by keeping reserves at the Federal Reserve (and don't need T-bills for yield), but T-bills finance government spending. So why push it in that direction? To push the fast-growing pool of digital dollar reserves toward Treasuries, creating steady new demand for public debt. In doing so, the Act reframed crypto not as a threat to the monetary system, but as a tool to strengthen it—by aligning digital dollar infrastructure with the fiscal needs of the US government. Other countries are expected to follow suit.

The law set clear, rigorous standards. Stablecoins had to be backed, dollar for dollar, by short-term US Treasuries or equivalent cash reserves. Issuers were required to publish real-time disclosures, undergo independent audits, and guarantee redemption rights for users. These weren't minor tweaks—they were the elements of institutional trust, applied to a technology that had long operated in the gray.

But what mattered most wasn't just the legal scaffolding. It was the story the law began to tell—A story in which blockchain wasn't there to replace the dollar—but to extend it.

As US Treasury Secretary Scott Bessent put it:

> Stablecoins represent a revolution in digital finance. The dollar now has an internet-native payment rail that is fast, frictionless, and free of middlemen. This groundbreaking technology will buttress the dollar's status as the global reserve currency, expand access to the dollar economy for billions across the globe, and lead to a surge in demand for U.S. Treasuries, which back stablecoins.[2]

Stablecoins—once dismissed as speculative instruments—are now being recognized as a means by which nations can advance their strategic interests and influence global affairs. And far from undermining the status quo, they may be what helps the dollar meet the demands of a networked, globalized economy.

Other Imaginative Use Cases

Beyond memes, stable payment methods, and the like, blockchains are powering entirely new kinds of markets. They are interesting because they are open, programmable, and operate at internet speed. I also think they are interesting both because of what they facilitate now and, even more so, because they are a first wave of building that shows a world of possibilities. I suspect, however, that the use cases that spawn the "killer apps" are still in development or perhaps haven't yet been conceived.

Among the most notable blockchain use cases today are perpetual futures and prediction markets. They already handle billions of dollars and are starting to impact how people trade, hedge, and even understand the world around them.

Perpetual futures, or "perps," are contracts that enable users to take long or short positions on the price of assets—crypto, stocks, commodities—without actually owning them. They are different from traditional futures in that they don't expire. Perps track prices continuously and settle in real time, with funding rates keeping them tethered to spot prices. Each month, billions in volume flow through decentralized perp exchanges such as dYdX, GMX, Hyperliquid, and Aster. Perp exchanges function without brokers or clearinghouses. They provide an interesting combination of access and autonomy: global, 24/7 markets governed by code, not gatekeepers.

Prediction markets offer a different kind of insight. Using platforms like Polymarket, users bet on real-world outcomes—from elections to economic data. The financial stakes lead to sharper forecasts. What was fascinating to watch during the 2024 U.S. presidential race was the way in which Polymarket odds were cited alongside major polls, and in some cases offered earlier or more accurate signals about shifting voter sentiment.

Beyond finance, one of the most imaginative frontiers is gaming. Why would you conceivably want a game to run "on-chain"? There are several reasons, the most compelling being that many gamers have spent large sums on in-game purchases and sometimes built their social lives around a game, only to find that the developer just switches it off. We are seeing a wave of blockchain game developers who use the democratic on-chain infrastructure to build games that are run by their players and can never be unilaterally switched off.

CHAPTER 15

The Integrity Web

I remember the first time I used the internet. The year was 1993. I was a student. I had a full head of hair and still thought I was more likely to go into standup than cryptography. The web was clunky, it felt novel, a bit weird. Interesting, yes. Useful? Not especially. I could look up the hours of a national park far away and send the odd email. Maybe the internet could be an occasional substitute for the library—or an alibi for why I wasn't in the library—but little more than that.

I think of this a lot when people say blockchain "sounds cool" but wonder what they'd actually use it for. I strongly believe we will look back to this time in history and realize that the question should have been "What won't we use it for?" Just like with the web, it will take us time to discover where blockchain fits in. That shouldn't surprise us because transformative technologies usually look trivial or unnecessary before their real use emerges.

In 1994, the bastion of tech journalism, *Wired*, was reporting that "companies want to do business on the Internet, but so far it's proven a tough target for spreadsheet jockeys."[1] Many just couldn't see the profit model. According to *Wired*, "Without accurate numbers indicating the Net's size and market potential, many firms investigating electronic commerce are reluctant to invest in net product development."[2] Websites and browsing, under the banner of the worldwide web, had been around for five years when these words were written, yet in another *Wired* article from the same year, it was stated that "everyone agrees that the Internet is the staging ground for the first true boom in electronic commerce, but it's a transactional wasteland."[3]

More than a decade later, applications that are now a part of everyday life were once dismissed as ridiculous. Take online food deliveries. In November 2007, when most of us were already living online, founders of a business called Hungryhouse pitched their business idea on *Dragons' Den*, the British version of Shark Tank. Customers could order different courses from different restaurants.

Panelist Deborah Meaden brushed it aside, saying, "Most people think, I fancy a Chinese [meal] tonight, or I fancy an Indian [meal] tonight. I don't think you go to a website and think, what do I want to eat tonight—so I'm out."[4]

That was the mood of the time. Hungryhouse found funding elsewhere, ended up partnering with more than 10,000 restaurants across Britain, and sold in 2018 for $260 million.

It's nearly impossible to predict how a sliver of activity—a percent of your day, an edge case—can swell until it defines the era.

Blockchain feels like it's in that early phase now. To most, transacting via blockchain still feels niche, experimental, maybe unnecessary. I am confident that just as the early internet hinted at more than anyone could articulate, blockchain points to a future where integrity is native to the web. Do I know exactly what we'll use it for? No, I have no idea—and I'm sure it'll be the last thing I can think of.

But do I know what the motivator will be? I'm as certain as I can be that it'll be the fact that blockchain is the best hope we have for integrity in human society and for honoring your autonomy or, as I like to put it, for enabling you to assert that you own your life.

Just as the early internet gave us the Information Age, blockchain is laying the foundation for the Integrity Web—an internet where trust is no longer assumed, but proven.

Integrity Web is the term I use to describe what I believe will emerge. It will almost certainly go by a different—and catchier—name. But whatever it's eventually called, its essence will be the same: a web where honesty and verifiability are built in.

And that is what this book has been about. Sure, it marvels at technology, and it's a love letter to math, and much more. But it is, fundamentally, about integrity and trust and the empowerment that it leads to. The innovations we've encountered—and in which I'm proud to have played a role—are remarkable in their technical brilliance. A blockchain is the equivalent of the stone into which truths were carved in antiquity, networked.

The goal is to create a world where trust prevails—a world built on math that is woven into the very fabric of everyday life.

You will recall, from early in the book, the three principles that are sacred to public blockchains. Broadness means anyone can participate. It refers to the absence of a velvet rope, not to the lack of special credentials. Follow the rules and you can help run the system. The second principle we encountered was public verifiability, which means that the rules and every action taken under them are open to inspection. Absolutely anyone can verify what happened, when, and how. The third principle we discussed, incentivized integrity, means that there are structural rewards for good behavior—we don't just hope for the best. Cheating is shooting yourself in the foot while acting fair earns you real returns.

Despite these ideals, blockchain technology is not a panacea. Like any human creation, it has limitations and vulnerabilities. Yet what it represents is a reordering of the foundations upon which interactions—personal, social, economic, and political—are built. From something as fleeting as a Facebook post to something as monumental as a multibillion-dollar international trade agreement, the way we define, verify, and preserve trust is being rewritten.

Old systems require us to blindly trust. Not just governments and banks, but also corporations so large and faceless that we can't even talk to them. Have you tried reaching a customer service department recently? You'll find yourself lost in phone menus or stuck with a chatbot. These are the very institutions to which we're expected to hand over our trust.

Banks illustrate the imbalance. They expect us to entrust them with our savings, yet they trust us so little that until recently they chained their pens to desks, worried we'd steal them. They make us book appointments and fill out forms to access our own money.

The problem doesn't come from malice; it comes from a concentration of power. By giving centralized entities more and more authority, we give away fragments of our own sovereignty. Old systems require faith; the new systems we're building have that trust encoded into their DNA, using the integrity of math.

That's why the academic paper that introduced STARKs to the world opens with these three words: "Human dignity demands . . ." It was the quest for dignity that fueled our research. It's what drove us to create the cryptographic proofs that shine a light in dark places, that level the playing field, and that restore human dignity by allowing anyone and everyone to assert their own integrity, to assert their own worth, and to enforce integrity on others. The scale that STARKs provide is, for me, all about scaling integrity, and the privacy they make possible is at the crux of human dignity.

Almost every transaction we do today involves a third party and, therefore, requires some element of trust. Paying cash for a hot dog from a street vendor is a rare exception. But any credit or debit card purchase, getting paid, renting an apartment, traveling, proving who you are—all depend on banks, registries, platforms, and institutions to carry out their side of the deal faithfully. Even storing a file or sending a message requires us to trust some remote, centralized actor to behave—to store it safely, not to peek, not to tamper, not to quietly extract value.

The internet has supercharged our dependency, and yet we have no real way to verify it. We tell ourselves the reputations of big institutions are too valuable to risk. And most of the time, we're right—until we're not. Even if they never violate our trust, their power comes at the expense of ours. And we pay for this weakness, in extra fees, in time, in limits put on our freedom, like the frustrating cases, every so often, when bank customers are told they can't move their own funds that are sitting in their own bank account.

To me, the great promise of crypto—and in particular, of blockchains—is that it gives us a way to do better. It offers a new kind of infrastructure, where trust isn't something you rely on Big Brother to supply, but something you can verify with respect to others (large or small), and where rules are public, enforcement is structural, and outcomes are guaranteed not by authority, but by math.

My hope isn't utopian; it's a technical possibility. Blockchain enables a digital world where integrity isn't optional, aspirational, or outsourced—it's the default. And it's not controlled by lofty centralized entities in marble buildings, but something anyone—large or small—can assert equally.

The only sustainable way to improve and maintain human dignity is to empower individuals and small communities, put them at the forefront, and give them real control over their economies and lives.

The deeper vision behind everything in this book is a future we call the *Integrity Web*—a new kind of internet infrastructure. It's one where the systems we rely on don't ask for our trust; they prove they deserve it.

In the rest of this chapter, I want to explore what that might mean. First, by painting a picture of what life could look like if this infrastructure were universal. Then by looking at how such a future might actually come to be. And finally, by reflecting on why I believe that the work my team and others are doing—especially on Starknet—will play a central role in making this infrastructure real.

The Empty Pot

I once told my kids an old Chinese story about an emperor looking for a successor.

He summons all the children of the kingdom and gives each one a pot with a single seed. "In a year's time," he says, "bring me what you've grown."

What the children don't know is that the seeds have been boiled. None of them can sprout.

A year later, they return to the palace, all but one of them proudly displaying a magnificent flower.

A single boy stands quietly with an empty pot. He had watered his seed faithfully, tended to it carefully, but nothing ever grew. Still, he brought back his pot exactly as it was.

The emperor chooses that boy as his heir.

My kids loved that story. I did too. And it's stayed with me because it's about a world where honesty is rewarded and deceit is exposed, whether it's by boiling seeds or by building cryptographic systems.

That's why the Integrity Web I envision matters so much. It's a web where honesty is systemic, not subjective. Honesty is built in, not enforced by moderators or intermediaries, but by code that no one can alter.

The Integrity Web: A New Kind of Infrastructure

Integrity Web is the name I'm using for something I think is already beginning to emerge. Ilia Volokh, a brilliant product manager at StarkWare, came up with the name and it's stuck in my head, and my imagination, ever since. As I see it, the Integrity Web is a new layer of the internet in which the systems we rely on aren't opaque vaults, but transparent mechanisms—where trust doesn't have to be blind.

This vision of an Integrity Web matters because today intermediaries sit in the middle of almost everything we do; even everyday acts like paying bills, claiming benefits, updating records, or posting online depend on opaque systems we didn't build, can't audit, and often shouldn't fully trust.

It's no longer safe to assume these systems are universally neutral and fair, and that's exactly where the Integrity Web comes in.

With blockchains and zero-knowledge proofs, we can build apps that prove they're doing what they say—without exposing private data. Once your vote is cast, no one can uncast it. Once a contract is agreed on, it can't be altered. Once your property deed is on-chain, no one can quietly rewrite it. The guarantees are baked in.

This need for verification becomes even more urgent when AI shapes what we see, what we believe, and how we act. The problem is that we don't know how it works. Maybe it's repeating a bias. Maybe it's reflecting an invisible sponsorship. Maybe it's tailored to silence one perspective and boost another. Everything is hidden inside the "black box."

With the Integrity Web, even AI would have to let us look under the hood, as Aggelos Kiayias suggested to Nathan in Chapter 6. The tools within AI—the apps or software we interact with—would have to reveal their data sources. Their models—the programs trained on data to recognize patterns and make decisions—would be anchored to a blockchain to prove that no tampering had occurred. If they claim neutrality, they have to prove it. If they provide advice, they must also offer a method for evaluating its origin.

The Integrity Web that I foresee is an ecosystem that will come together gradually, piece by piece: tools that show your funds are safe, registries that prove no edits were made, and apps that demonstrate they're playing fair.

This revolution won't arrive overnight. It will begin as a quiet but profound shift in what we expect from the systems that ask for our trust. In years to come, I believe we'll look back at how blindly we trusted opaque institutions and wonder how we could have been so careless. Our task now is to turn that new expectation into reality by actually rolling out systems that can prove their integrity.

How the Integrity Web Will Emerge

The Integrity Web will emerge organically to meet real-world needs, much like other flavors of the internet we have met until today. Nobody will impose blockchain on people. They'll embrace it as and when it does the things they need it to do. Blockchain will take shape piece by piece, through countless individual efforts and innovations. STARKs are one of those innovations. At StarkWare, the company I co-founded, we built Starknet as a place for developers to experiment at the boundaries of this new infrastructure.

On Starknet, developers can build apps that are fast, scalable, and provably fair. Starknet isn't the only network of this kind, nor should it be. The Integrity Web won't live on any one chain. However, I do believe that Starknet can be one of the places where this vision takes root. Starknet will offer privacy and connect securely to other blockchains including Bitcoin and, I expect, the privacy-focused Zcash that I have discussed.

Starknet doesn't just scale blockchains like Bitcoin and Ethereum—it unlocks something entirely new. Because of the unique way it's built, it gives anyone—regardless of credentials or background—the power to run their own market, auction house, or exchange. No gatekeepers. No barriers to entry. Just code.

And here's the twist, which we discussed in Chapter 12: all these independently run marketplaces can operate in parallel—serving different communities or purposes—yet still settle safely and securely on Starknet. It's like recreating the pre-internet world of commerce, where many local economies ran side by side, constantly cross-settling, merging, and evolving. Starknet brings that richness and flexibility into the blockchain era.

Already, I see people using Starknet to build things that just wouldn't be possible on traditional infrastructure—apps where users don't just click "I agree," but where they can check exactly what they're agreeing to. This approach goes beyond simply reviewing the terms and conditions. It means confirming that the code running on the blockchain does exactly what it claims to do, through systems where rules are enforced not by some hidden server logic, but by transparent code. Tools for digital identity, voting, finance, and games are all being shaped with integrity as a core feature, not an afterthought.

On a daily basis, I use a wallet app built on Starknet, which is essentially the blockchain equivalent of a bank. During one of my longer foreign trips, I tried to organize my banking with local banks to serve my needs, but I was constantly blocked from the uses I needed. As Nathan described in Chapter 9, his debit card produced by Ready, a company run by Starknet pioneers Itamar Lesuisse and Julien Niset, never stops working. It automatically exchanges crypto for my purchases in any currency, and so long as he has the funds, his transactions are never refused. It's crypto in the real world, without prohibitive transaction fees thanks to the very STARK cryptography I co-invented.

While I am discussing Starknet here, the broad movement to build public, verifiable blockchain infrastructure is much larger than any single network, and it needs to be so for the Integrity Web to evolve. Developers are utilizing other blockchains—such as Zcash, Ethereum, Solana, and Bitcoin itself—to anchor truth in public, verifiable ways. They're experimenting with decentralized social media and reputation systems, where trust is earned rather than extracted, and with always-open markets: prediction platforms, perpetual exchanges, and other tools that don't shut down when the office lights go out.

I feel fortunate to be among the team members working on this Integrity Web vision. Through Starknet, open-source research, and collaboration with others across the ecosystem, I aim to help grow the Integrity Web not as a product, but as a public good. It's not a blockchain revolution. It's a human one.

Interest Will Grow

We've heard it all before, and it's easy to roll your eyes—another big vision on how tech will help the world. Many of these visions have actually made things worse. Dreams of free and open communication have been shattered by corporate greed. But I don't think this is the story of blockchain. I don't think the Integrity Web is some idealist fantasy.

First, how many of these other premises have been built on a genuine democratizing movement, on infrastructure that is decentralized (owned by everyone and by no one). And second, I'm convinced that blockchain represents a practical answer to a real need. We were promised a digital commons where we could wander freely, and we ended up with something that feels more like a very intricate maze.

The Integrity Web isn't a vague hope for the distant future. It's happening in the here and now. I've met developers from Argentina who are paying workers in stablecoins because the peso, their local currency, is collapsing. Students in Nigeria are putting their credentials on-chain so they won't disappear if the regime changes. Engineers are turning math into something ordinary people can use—not because it's trendy, but because it works.

I'm excited about the idealism of the Integrity Web. But I'm realistic enough to understand that most people will appreciate the fact that it's useful, rather than the fact that it's decentralized.

Once apps become fast, affordable, and easy to use, people will switch. In doing so, they will reclaim control of their digital lives from the faceless corporations that currently act as self-appointed custodians. As we said at the outset, history will tell a single story about the combined evolution of the internet and blockchain. In time, we'll no longer distinguish one from the other because, together, they will provide the substrate for all our online activity. Blockchain will fade into the background, much like the early web did. What will emerge is a society in which individuals are empowered and the overlords of the digital world are placed in check.

Own Your Life

There's a phrase I use about blockchain that makes people think I'm being too dramatic. I say that blockchain is about "owning your life." And it is. Not only owning your life, but owning your community.

For decades we've handed trust away from communities we could see and touch—religious groups, neighborhood clubs, circles of friends—and toward faceless centralized entities. The internet made the world smaller, but in the process it hollowed out local bonds and left us instead trying to prove to a CAPTCHA robot that we are human.

The pandemic made that hollowing visible. Think back to lockdown. Who benefited? As the coffers of actual community meeting places dried up—local social centers, religious buildings, your community café—businesses that extract value out of your interactions with friends saw their revenue soar. With every frustrated post and cabin-fever video we uploaded, the social media platforms blasted our contacts with more and more ads.

Platforms like TikTok and YouTube fed us whatever was trending inside echo chambers. Voices of real communities—friends, neighbors, teachers, shopkeepers—were often drowned out by influencers and alarmists.

The pandemic was a weird time. Day-to-day connections shrank. In their place, we had a dystopian feed: Big Brother flooding us with videos, algorithms nudging us toward outrage and deciding what reality looked like. Institutions we relied on in the physical world—town halls, clubs, even families—proved fragile online. Those who held power in the digital space could be disingenuous, and often were.

The pandemic held up a mirror to our online life as so much else faded away. It was fascinating because on the one hand it showed us how much social platforms bind us. But on the other, it showed us all that is wrong. And it made many of us think more deeply about blockchain. Not networks where we are users, but networks where we are stakeholders. Digital tools are now at the disposal of communities themselves—to unite online in ways that work best for them, to build together, and to interact on their own terms.

That's what I mean by "owning your life." Yes, owning your money in ways banks can't block you, but much more than that. Owning the value that flows from your life, whether it be your salary or your comic video.

We've seen some glimpses of an interesting future in projects like Gitcoin Grants, where thousands of ordinary people have pooled resources to fund open-source software, climate action, and local community work. I expect to see such initiatives grow, and to see communities using digital rails to direct capital and energy toward the public goods they care about most.

The functionality of blockchain is transformative in many everyday situations, including how families handle money. Imagine you're a wealthy uncle, and your nephew wants to buy a home. You'd be more than happy to lend him money—after all, why not have interest paid to you rather than to a bank? The real hurdle is what happens if he stops making the agreed repayments and the relationship becomes awkward. With a blockchain-based smart contract, you can both agree in advance on the repayment schedule and the consequences of missing a payment, and the code will automatically enforce those terms. Every last detail of the family loan—amounts, dates, and remedies—can be baked into the contract.

As you will sense, I am excited about a deeper revolution: not coins, not contracts, but the chance to shift trust back from remote authorities to systems we govern ourselves. Blockchain won't recreate the church hall or the sports club, but it can let us design digital spaces with the same integrity—places where voices aren't lost in the noise of influencers, where communities can pool resources without intermediaries, and where rules are shaped by the community itself.

My Role in This Story

What I love about blockchain is that it feels like so much more than technology. At its best, it is a meeting place between mathematics, philosophy, economics, and human aspiration—a way of turning abstract ideas about truth and fairness into something people can actually touch.

Starknet is, for me, so much more than just another blockchain network. It has become a practical laboratory where the hidden beauty of math is brought out into the open. For most of my career, that beauty was barely noticed outside a narrow circle of academics sufficiently well-versed in the math needed to appreciate it. What excites me now is seeing those same ideas—once so disconnected from daily life—translated into systems that are visible, usable, and impactful.

STARK proofs, reared by hand in the comfortable world of academia, have been released into the wild, where they are not just fending for themselves, but are positively thriving. They allow many thousands of people to transact, create, and collaborate without having to blindly trust one another. The math itself, uncompromising and transparent, guarantees the fairness of the system. What was once a hidden symmetry on a whiteboard becomes a living architecture that anyone can use. The aesthetic elegance of a zero-knowledge proof has been transformed into a public utility.

But this project is not a solitary one. Starknet is my corner of a much larger story, of the emerging Integrity Web. And what makes this story so moving is the community it gathers. At blockchain events—many of them wonderfully strange, full of outsiders—you find an inversion of the old hierarchies. Great ideas don't come only from prestigious universities or big-name labs. They come from teenagers teaching themselves to code, from developers in places ignored by the old tech world, from people without formal credentials but with a burning sense of what could be different. I watch, marveling at the sight of mathematics becoming visible to the world, not as an abstraction, but as a lived reality. The real thrill is seeing that my own research has become the foundation for evolving technologies that are beyond my understanding.

Blockchain Is Too Important to Become Politicized

Is music left-wing or right-wing? Plumbing? Cloud computing?

Of course not. These are absurd questions—yet we find ourselves asking them about blockchain. In recent years, especially during the US election in 2024, blockchain became a political flashpoint. The right largely embraced it; the left mostly recoiled. Without warning, a sophisticated technology—at its core, an advanced database—became caught in a tug-of-war.

Here's the point: Blockchain is not a creature of the right or the left. It is not inherently anti-regulation or pro-redistribution. It is not a political philosophy; it is infrastructure—flexible, adaptable, and pluralistic.

Technologies are not political by nature. They become political by use, by narrative, and by timing. Blockchain, like the internet before it, must be judged not by the ideology of its early adopters, but by the architecture it enables and the agency it restores. It's about empowering individuals with real sovereignty, strengthening communities, and weakening monopolies.

Make no mistake: Libertarian ideals had a real and lasting impact on crypto's early development. Many saw blockchain as a tool to bypass state control. But like any technology, it must outgrow its origins. The internet did the same. It, too, began in fringe communities—first academic, then military—before becoming global infrastructure.

Language shapes perception. Crypto, once shorthand for cryptography, now carries baggage. Blockchain still suggests systems, infrastructure, possibility. What it lacks is urgency—a sense of "I need that," a sense that it speaks to real human needs. But that, too, is starting to shift.

I believe blockchain, paired with the kind of narrative we've begun to build in this book, is laying the groundwork for something broader and more vital—something like the Integrity Web.

So the real issue isn't just the architecture—it's also the narrative. It's time to separate blockchain's promise from its PR problems because blockchain must transcend political divisions; no political camp can afford to be left out while the digital backbone of the future is being laid.

Despite these difficulties, there are reasons to be optimistic. The passage of the 2025 Genius Act in the United States—the country's first comprehensive regulatory framework for stablecoins—won bipartisan support. In Ukraine, blockchain, as used in the government's Diia platform, has become a digital lifeline, especially for those displaced by the conflict. In Bhutan, state-led Bitcoin mining has cross-party backing and is viewed not as speculation, but as a means to harness hydroelectric power and bolster the country's economic strength.

At its core, blockchain is a powerful tool. Its value depends on who wields it and how they wield it. The question is not who owns it, but who builds with it, and what they build to benefit humanity. That question is no longer just about technology; it's about the kind of world, digital and otherwise, that we choose to build. Nathan and I hope that you carry with you the vision of an Integrity Web—a new kind of internet where honesty is built in, where trust is no longer fragile, and where integrity is guaranteed by design.

So that you own your life.

Appendix

Questions About STARK Proofs Answered

What is a Proof in the Context of STARK Proofs and Blockchain Systems?

A proof demonstrates that a computer performed a complex calculation (or computation) correctly, meaning each and every step was carried out exactly according to the rules of the program. For example, if we add 5 and 3, the result must be 8 and not 7.999999999. A computation can be made of billions of such steps, and one stray digit—by intention or mistake—can have disastrous (and expensive) consequences. A small error in a calculation for medicine or the program running a pacemaker could cost lives.

A proof attests to the correctness of a much longer mathematical process, so there's no need to check every step individually. Verifying the proof guarantees that all steps followed the rules.

What is Computation?

Computation just means following a set of steps—taking some input data, following a list of instructions (a program), and producing an output. Computation could be a computer crunching numbers or a human working through a calculation by hand—slowly but surely. What matters is that the process is well-defined and repeatable: clear instructions, clear result.

Sending money, checking a password, sorting numbers, and processing images—all of these are computations.

Examples of computations:

1. A payment app checks your balance.
2. A smart contract calculates what you're owed.
3. A game engine figures out your next move.

STARKs help when these computations are big and messy. Imagine a bank's end-of-month report with 10,000 individual line items. Instead of rechecking every entry to confirm the totals, STARKs provide a proof that the entire computation was done honestly. This proof is generated by a process that verifies every step of the computation internally, then compresses the guarantee of correctness into a small package. The verifier can check this package quickly and efficiently, instead of reviewing every step.

What's the Big Idea Behind STARKs?

To best explain how STARKs work, let's picture a visit to a public swimming pool. This explanation has been cited earlier in the book, but is included here for those who may be checking this appendix before reaching that point.

As described in Chapter 8, we can compare this to a swimming pool test. You arrive at the pool, just as a group of 200 toddlers is leaving. You do the math in your head: What are the odds none of them had a little accident? Nobody wants to swim in contaminated water—but testing every drop is impossible.

So the pool staff run a chemical test, adding a few drops of solution to a sample of pool water. It changes color if there's any contamination. They don't need to test the whole pool because the solution is so sensitive it picks up even the tiniest trace.

STARKs work in a very similar way—but for big computer tasks.

If someone tampers with a huge computation, like slipping a zero into a transaction to commit fraud, a STARK proof will catch it. Like the water test, it can do that by randomly sampling just a few "drops" of the computation—not even a full step.

Here's the kicker: In a real pool, contamination might stay in one corner. But STARKs are like a high-speed current that mixes everything instantly. If there's any dirt, it spreads. So checking just a few spots is enough to know if there's a problem. No hiding places. No blind spots. That's the power of STARKs: small samples, big truth.

The STARK prover is the current, and the verifier is the staff member who samples the water. We'll explain exactly what the prover and verifier do in a later section. If anything's off, the proof almost certainly fails. (The prover commits to the full computation; the verifier performs randomized checks on its encoding.) And posting the proof to the blockchain is like pinning the water test results on the pool notice board.

Here's how the analogy maps to the actual machinery of STARKs:

- The pool = the full computation—often massive, with millions of steps.
- Contamination = an error or fraud in the computation (e.g., dishonest output).
- The chemical test = the verifier's sampling check.
- The high-speed current = the prover's encoding of the computation as a set of numbers.
- This spreads any error across the entire domain—so even local mistakes affect the whole.
- The water sample = a handful of randomly chosen points that the verifier checks, via constraint testing and proximity testing.
- Sensitivity = the soundness error—a key property of STARKs, which guarantees that if something's wrong, the odds of a bad proof passing the test are astronomically low.
- Posting results on the notice board = putting the STARK proof on-chain. It's public, tamper-proof, and efficient to verify.

Together, these elements make STARKs a trustless, scalable way to publicly prove that a computation was done correctly—without having to redo it. That's the essence of what this technology enables.

DELVING A BIT DEEPER

In the analogy above, we saw how STARKs catch errors like testing a few drops of pool water. Now, let's explore how that analogy maps to the actual computation process in more technical terms.

In blockchain, STARKs prove that a batch of transactions—say, a million—correctly changes the system's state from A to B. A prover (e.g., block proposer) constructs the proof, and the rest of the network (verifiers) checks it. The result is trustless validation that doesn't require inspecting each transaction.

Instead of each node redoing all computations (as in Bitcoin or Ethereum), nodes verify a succinct proof. The key advantage: verifying a STARK proof is exponentially faster than processing the transactions themselves.

Step 1: The prover records every execution step from all transactions as a sequence of numbers. Each step must obey rules or constraints, like a Sudoku puzzle where every number placement must satisfy specific conditions.

Step 2: The prover expands the sequence using error-detection methods similar to check digits. These additions, known as error-correcting codes, link many parts of the data together.

As a result, one small error ripples outward, disrupting many values. Cheating becomes nearly impossible: a single wrong entry spoils the consistency of the entire structure.

STARKs use Reed-Solomon codes, based on low-degree polynomials. These make it mathematically certain that even tiny errors throw everything off. So the verifier can inspect just a few random spots and be confident the full computation was correct—even if it had billions of steps.

What About Privacy?

The pool analogy that we discussed above gets us far. It captures one of STARKs' core strengths: scalability. You don't need to test every drop of water to know the pool is clean—just a few samples are enough. That's how STARKs help blockchains stay fast and efficient: by compressing enormous computations into compact, verifiable proofs.

But STARKs have a second superpower the pool can't show. That superpower is privacy.

STARKs let you prove that a computation was done correctly—without revealing the sensitive data behind it. The logic was followed. The output checks out. But the inputs, the intermediate steps, even the result itself—all of that can stay hidden.

Think of it like this: Instead of proving the pool is clean, now you want to prove you took a swim—but not say when, where, or with whom. Or you want to prove you're old enough to buy alcohol from the poolside bar, without disclosing your exact birthdate. That's the shift from scale to privacy.

It's not about secrecy for its own sake. It's about control—control over what's shared and what stays private. You decide what to reveal and what to keep hidden.

This flexibility opens doors far beyond blockchain—into areas like identity, healthcare, voting, and secure access. Whenever privacy and correctness need to coexist, STARKs offer a way.

What is Zero Knowledge?

Zero knowledge is the principle that makes privacy in STARKs possible. It means proving a statement is true—without revealing why it's true or what makes it so.

Say you want to prove you know the password to an account, but don't want to reveal the password itself. A zero-knowledge proof lets you do exactly that: Show you know it, without disclosing a single character.

It's like holding up a sealed envelope with the answer inside. You're showing you've got the goods—but no one gets to peek.

STARKs are capable of this kind of privacy by design. But here's the powerful part: They don't require it. If privacy isn't needed—say, when publishing a public audit or verifying open data—STARKs can run in full transparency. No secrecy, just correctness.

So STARKs are flexible: Want privacy? Keep the data hidden. Just need to prove it was done right? Keep it public and save resources.

It's not one-size-fits-all. STARKs adapt to the job—whether the priority is privacy, scale, or both.

Why Move Computation off the Blockchain?

Blockchains are like meticulous librarians. They check every single step of every transaction to make sure nothing fishy gets through. That's great for honesty—but terrible for speed.

Every computer (or node) on the network has to rework every step. That's like asking every shop in your city to individually verify your receipt every time you buy a coffee. It's expensive, it's slow, and it doesn't scale.

STARKs flip the script.

Working directly on a blockchain is like renting real estate in Manhattan—impossibly expensive—because every step of every transaction has to be checked by every node.

With STARKs, one party—the prover—goes off and does the heavy lifting in Oklahoma, where it's cheaper.

The prover then brings back a cryptographic proof that says, "Here's what I did, and I can mathematically prove it was all done by the book."

No shortcuts. No special pleading. Just math.

This approach makes blockchains faster, cheaper, and more scalable—without giving up on trust. The proof is airtight. If someone tried to sneak in a fake transaction—like giving $1 million of somebody else's money—the proof wouldn't pass. The cheat would be caught. It's that simple.

The beauty? STARKs let us move work away from the high-rent blockchain to the low-rent equivalent of an out-of-town industrial zone. The hard work is done off-chain, the proof is off-chain, but the trust stays on-chain.

What is a Prover?

The prover is the worker bee—the machine (or cluster of machines) doing the computing, the job we actually care about.

Say we've got a million transactions to process. The prover runs through all of them, follows the program line by line, and comes out the other side with an updated state of the system. It's like a really careful accountant who recalculates every number from scratch.

But here's the catch: We don't trust the prover.

The prover could be honest, or it could be a smooth-talking liar. So we ask it to generate a STARK proof—a short, rigorous summary that shows it played fair.

Technically, the prover takes:

- A claim: "This is what I did."
- The witness data: all the detailed information about each step in the computation.

Then it crunches all that into a STARK proof—a kind of cryptographic receipt that anyone can verify.

Who is the prover in practice? It could be a blockchain node, a cloud server, or a specialized off-chain machine, but it doesn't matter. What matters is the proof. If the math checks out, the work stands.

What is a Verifier?

The verifier is the checker. It's the skeptical one—the party that says, "Okay, prove it."

Verifiers don't see all the messy details. They don't redo the work. Instead, they run a few clever mathematical checks on the STARK proof and make a decision: pass or fail. Think of it as the world's smartest bouncer—it doesn't check the whole party, but it can instantly sniff out a fake invite.

The verifier gets:

- The claim: for example, "This is the new state of the system."
- The proof: the cryptographic summary created by the prover.

Then it runs fast, random spot-checks that are mathematically designed to catch even the tiniest lie or mistake. Whether sloppy or fraudulent, the verifier will catch it—with overwhelming probability.

Verifiers are lightweight, efficient, and decentralized. A blockchain can be the verifier. So can a mobile phone, a laptop, or a toaster (okay, maybe not the toaster—but you get the idea).

The big deal? Verifiers can check a massive job in a few milliseconds. That speed is what lets STARKs scale blockchains without sacrificing trust. It's math doing the job of a thousand eyes.

What Can and Can't be Proved?

Let's start with what can't be proved.

STARKs can't tell you if a painting is beautiful. They can't prove love, fairness, or what someone meant. There's no "zero-knowledge proof of good vibes."

What they can prove is whether a computer followed the rules.

Did the computer run a program correctly? Did it sort a list, process transactions, or update a game state—for example, the positions of all pieces in an online game—by the book, meaning by the declared rules? That's where STARKs shine.

If the task is well-defined—like a recipe with clear steps—then a STARK can prove it was followed without needing to see every ingredient.

Formally, STARKs can handle anything in a class of computations called NEXP (nondeterministic exponential time). That's computer science talk for: "If you can describe what the program does, and how many steps it should take, then we can generate a proof for it."

This class of computations covers just about every real-world scenario you'd want to verify:

- Smart contracts that run on a blockchain like Ethereum
- Financial transactions
- Game logic in online games
- Scientific simulations
- Digital identity checks
- Artificial intelligence

If a computer can do it—and do it step by step—a STARK can prove it did it right.

What Resources does it Take to Create a STARK Proof?

Creating a STARK proof is heavy lifting. We're talking serious computing power. Think CPU cycles churning, memory juggling, and temporary storage buzzing—all working together like a busy kitchen coordinating its stoves, ovens, and prep areas.

Let's say the number of steps to run a task—like processing a day's worth of transactions—is T. That means the computer has to perform T small operations, one after another.

To generate a STARK proof for that task, the prover (the one doing the work) needs to do roughly T × log(T) steps. So what's log(T)?

It's a mathematical way of measuring how big a number is—not by its exact value, but by how many digits it takes to write it down. So log(T) doesn't care about the exact number; it cares about how many digits it takes to write the number down, how many zeroes there would be if you rounded it to the nearest power of 10.

Questions About STARK Proofs Answered

For example:

$$1{,}000 \text{ has } 4 \text{ digits} \rightarrow \log(1{,}000) \text{ is about } 3$$

$$1{,}000{,}000 \text{ has } 7 \text{ digits} \rightarrow \log(1{,}000{,}000) \text{ is about } 6$$

$$1{,}000{,}000{,}000{,}000 \text{ (a trillion) has } 13 \text{ digits} \rightarrow \log(1{,}000{,}000{,}000{,}000)$$
$$\text{is about } 12$$

So, let's say your original task takes a trillion steps to run.

The prover will need to do around 12 trillion steps to create a proof.

Remember, log(T) is the number of zeroes in T. In our case T is 1,000,000,000,000. It has 12 zeroes, so log(T) is 12. And so:

$$T \times \log(T) = 12{,}000{,}000{,}000{,}000.$$

That's a lot, a dozen-fold more steps than running the computation, but it only has to be done once. It's still way more efficient than having every other participant re-run the whole trillion-step process themselves.

And here's the magic of STARKs: the harder a computation is to prove, the more efficient it is to check.

As we mentioned earlier, and will be mentioned below, the prover finishes their work and produces the proof; anyone else can verify it using just log(T) steps—in our example, about 12 steps.

This is what makes STARKs so powerful. You pay a big upfront cost to prove the work—in this case, 12 times as many steps as the original—but after that, verifying it is practically free. It's a one-time effort that unlocks effortless trust for everyone else.

What's the Speed Advantage of Using STARKs?

As a reminder from above, one of STARKs' biggest strengths is verification speed. Verifiers don't need to redo the original work—they just check a tiny mathematical proof. Let's see how that plays out.

Say 1 million transactions need to be verified. Normally, every computer (node) in the network has to re-run all 1 million transactions to be sure they're valid. That's slow, expensive, and doesn't scale well.

Now enter STARKs.

With a STARK, you process those 1 million transactions off-chain and produce one short proof that says, "Yes, all of these were processed correctly."

Then, instead of redoing all the work, the blockchain just has to verify the proof—a quick check, like scanning a barcode. Using the T × log(T) formula, the prover did about 6 million steps. The verifier has to do about 6.

What Kind of Cryptography is Behind STARKs?

Although STARKs sound like science fiction, they are built on very real, very solid cryptography. What kind exactly? Or to put the question more precisely, what basic cryptographic building blocks do STARKs require?

At the heart of it all is the humble hash function. If you've ever used a password manager, sent a secure message, or visited a secure website with HTTPS (almost all websites today use HTTPS), you've relied on a hash function. It's a kind of digital fingerprint: It takes in data (no matter how big), scrambles it in a specific way, and spits it out as a string of characters like this: f7c3bc1d808e04732adf679965 ccc34ca7ae3441e5b7f3a6a7a1a39a7b8543e1.

Hash functions are simple, widely used, and—most importantly—hard to mess with. Change even one pixel in a photo, and the output changes completely. And it's practically impossible to reverse-engineer what the input was, just by looking at the output.

STARKs use hash functions (plus some clever math from algebra and probability) to commit to a huge amount of computation via a short string using a cryptographic structure called a Merkle tree—and to do it without needing any secret setup. That's what makes them transparent: no need for The Ceremony, there are no special keys, no trust assumptions. Just battle tested cryptography, done right.

Why are STARKs Secure—Even Against Quantum Computers?

Quantum computers are no longer hypothetical. While the concept was once confined to labs and theory papers, they're now moving into reality. And they are vastly different to what we know as computers today. Unlike regular computers that try one solution at a time, quantum computers explore countless possibilities at once.

Think of them as solving a maze by testing every path in parallel and keeping only the one that leads to the exit.

This could break much of today's cryptography. If I had a regular computer trying to find the seed phrase, which is the master key protecting your Bitcoin wallet, it would take longer than the age of the universe to guess it. A quantum machine could someday crack it in minutes. The good news? Not all cryptography is vulnerable.

ZK-STARKs—the zero-knowledge proofs I co-invented, which are discussed in this book and which underpin Starknet—are built differently. They don't rely on fragile mathematical assumptions like factoring or elliptic curves, which quantum algorithms can break. Instead, their security depends only on hash functions, which remain strong even in the quantum era.

Why does any of this matter? It matters because cryptography underpins our entire digital economy. As quantum power grows, most systems will need to be rebuilt. But ZK-STARKs are already future-proof.

They don't just survive quantum threats. They were designed to outlast them.

What is Soundness?

Soundness is a measure of the safety of a cryptographic system. In our case, it's a measure of the safety of a STARK. It's a number, usually a very small number, like 1 in 10 to the power of 30. What this number means can be explained in two different ways: if you try to fake a STARK—like winning a lottery—it's the probability that you'll be lucky. It's a very small number. Alternatively, if you work hard, like the *Charlie and the Chocolate Factory* character, and try again and again—even assuming you can try a million times per second—it'll take you, on average, 10 to the power of 13 years to find a fake STARK, whereas the sun will run cold in about 10 to the power of 10 years.

Where did STARKs Come From?

STARKs didn't just appear out of nowhere—they're the product of more than 40 years of transformative academic work in cryptography and computer science.[1]

It started in the mid-1980s, when Shafi Goldwasser, Silvio Micali, and Charles Rackoff introduced the idea of interactive proofs and zero-knowledge proofs—ways to verify information without revealing it. Oded Goldreich, Silvio Micali, and Avi Wigderson (my PhD advisor) showed that zero-knowledge proofs apply to a wide range of problems—specifically, those in the complexity class known as NP. NP stands for "nondeterministic polynomial time"—problems where solutions are hard to find but easy to verify, like checking whether a filled Sudoku board is valid.

Then came the PCP (Probabilistically Checkable Proofs) revolution by a number of researchers spanning several works—Sanjeev Arora, László Babai, Lance Fortnow, Leonid Levin, Carsten Lund, Rajeev Motwani, Madhu Sudan (my Postdoc host), Mario Szegedy, and Muli Safra: a breakthrough showing that you can verify even huge computations by checking just a few random parts—no need to re-run the whole thing. Over the years PCPs have been made shorter and more efficient, and the starting point for my own work was a particularly efficient PCP system that I developed with Madhu Sudan in the early 2000s. Building on that, and together with my colleagues (most notably Alessandro Chiesa, my co-founder for Zcash and StarkWare) and students we developed efficient Interactive Oracle Proofs (IOPs): streamlined, highly efficient "conversations" between prover and verifier that organize those tiny checks. A key component that drove efficiency was the Fast RS IOP (FRI) protocol which I co-authored with three of my students, and which underlies the efficiency of most practical STARKs today.

STARKs bring all these ideas into the real world. They combine:

- PCPs, to let us check massive jobs with tiny tests
- IOPs that facilitate efficient conversations between prover and verifier
- Clever use of hash functions, for airtight security without needing any secret setup

The result is a proof system that's:

- Scalable (handles massive computations)
- Transparent (no hidden keys or trusted setup)
- Post-quantum secure (safe even from future quantum computers)

STARKs are the culmination of decades of theory, now powering real-world systems like StarkEx and Starknet—and helping build the secure infrastructure of the future.

Are STARKs Relevant Only to Blockchains?

Not at all.

STARKs are making headlines in blockchain because that's where the need is greatest: scaling systems, slashing costs, and keeping things honest—all without trust. But their potential goes way beyond crypto.

At their core, STARKs are about proving that complex computations were done correctly—without needing to redo them. That's useful for anything we care about:

- Privacy
- Integrity
- Speed
- Having confidence in the result, without needing to trust the person who did the work

Think: secure voting, private medical data, scientific simulations, AI auditing, cloud computing, even multiplayer gaming. And these are just a few small examples. If a system runs complex logic and others need to trust the result, STARKs can help.

Why haven't we seen STARKs in all those places yet? Because blockchain happened to be the first mainstream problem that screamed out for this kind of solution. But the rest? That's another story . . . and maybe another book. For now, what matters is this: STARKs let us trust results—not people.

Glossary

This glossary brings together the key ideas, terms, and tools we discuss throughout the book. Each entry explains the concept in plain language and connects it to how blockchain systems work in practice. Whether you're meeting these ideas for the first time or just revisiting a chapter, this glossary has you covered.

Bitcoin   The first digital currency that works without banks.

Block   A "page" in the blockchain that holds recent transactions.

Blockchain   A shared digital record that anyone can view and verify. It stores data in blocks linked together so that no one can secretly change the past.

Circle USD (USDC)   A regulated US dollar stablecoin issued by the company Circle.

Coin   The main currency of a blockchain, such as Bitcoin (BTC) or Ether (ETH).

Consensus   The process by which all nodes agree on what's true.

dApp (Decentralized App)   An application built on blockchain that no single company controls.

Decentralization   Power that is spread out. That way, no single company controls it.

Decentralized Autonomous Organization (DAO)   An online group that makes decisions using blockchain votes and smart contracts.

Double-Spend Problem   How to stop someone from sending the same digital coin twice; something Bitcoin solved with consensus.

Ethereum   A blockchain that lets anyone run code and build applications as well as send money.

Feature, Not a Bug   The idea that blockchain's slowness is intentional to stay secure and open to everyone.

51% Attack   When one group controls most of the mining power and could alter transactions.

Finality   Once confirmed and on-chain, a transaction is effectively irreversible.

Gas Fee   A small fee paid to run or record actions on Ethereum, Starknet, and some other blockchains.

GENIUS Act (2025)   A US law requiring stablecoins to hold full cash or Treasury reserves and publish audits. It made stablecoins part of mainstream finance.

Governance   How blockchain users make decisions and set rules together.

Glossary

Hard Cap Bitcoin's total supply limit of 21 million coins.

Immutability Once added, records cannot be changed without detection.

Incentivized Integrity Honest behavior gets rewarded, while cheating wastes money and power.

Interactive Proof A back-and-forth process where the verifier asks the prover questions to check correctness of a computation or mathematical statement.

Latency How long a transaction takes to be confirmed to reach finality.

Layer 2 (L2) A system that handles most activity off the main blockchain and sends final results back to the main blockchain, making things faster and cheaper.

Ledger The full record of all transactions on the blockchain.

Mining Running powerful computers to perform PoW and earn new coins.

Nakamoto, Satoshi The unknown creator of Bitcoin, active until 2010.

Node A computer that helps run and check the blockchain.

Open-Source Protocol Public code anyone can read, use, or improve.

Probabilistically Checkable Proof (PCP) A format for writing proofs that can be checked for correctness by polling (examining) only small random parts of the proof.

Proof of Work (PoW) A process where computers solve puzzles to secure the network and add blocks. This effort is known as "work" and consumes electricity. This is the system that keeps Bitcoin honest.

Prover The one who performs work and creates the proof in an interactive proof protocol.

Scalability How well a blockchain handles more users and activity without slowing down, becoming too expensive or compromising values of blockchain.

Scaling Trilemma A design trade-off: You can usually have only two of three—security, decentralization, and high speed.

Self-Custody Keeping your own private keys and controlling your funds directly.

Smart Contract Code on the blockchain that runs automatically when conditions are met. Example: Pay a driver only after a ride is confirmed.

Stablecoin A digital coin designed to stay at a fixed value, usually $1. It combines blockchain speed with the stability of fiat currencies.

Stakeholder Economy A system where users also share in ownership and profits, not just use the service.

Succinct Verification Checking huge amounts of data exponentially quickly by verifying one small proof instead of every detail.

Tether (USDT) One of the first and biggest US dollar-backed stablecoins.

Throughput (TPS) Transactions per second (TPS); how many transactions the network can process.

Token A digital item that can represent money, votes, or ownership.

Transparency Everything being open to public inspection.

Trusted Setup A one-time process that creates secret data needed for some proof systems (like ZK-SNARKs). If misused, it can break security. STARKs avoid this risk by not needing one.

Validity Proof Math and cryptography using interactive protocols and randomness to prove that a result was computed correctly without redoing all the work. It helps blockchains run faster and stay secure.

Verifier The one who checks the proof and confirms it's valid in an interactive proof protocol.

World Computer The idea that Ethereum acts like one shared global computer.

Zero-Knowledge Proof (ZKP) A class of interactive cryptographic proofs that show something is true without revealing private details. Example = proving you're over 18 without showing your date of birth.

ZK-SNARK A short, private one-step ZK proof used in Zcash and other blockchains. Many SNARKs require a trusted setup—an initial step where secret parameters are generated and later discarded. Full name—Succinct Non-Interactive ARgument of Knowledge.

ZK-STARK A newer class of proof systems used by Starknet and several other blockchains. STARKs eliminate the need for trusted setup and use cryptography that is secure against quantum attacks. Full name—Scalable Transparent ARgument of Knowledge.

Notes

Chapter 5: Beyond Currency: Blockchain as Infrastructure

1. All Magri quotations: Dr. Bernardo Magri, Department of Computer Science, University of Manchester, interviewed by Nathan Jeffay, Manchester, England, July 28, 2025.
2. All Casares quotations: Wences Casares, interviewed by Laura Shin, *Unchained* podcast, December 25, 2018.

Chapter 6: Social Media, AI, and the Gig Economy

1. All Kiayias quotations: Professor Aggelos Kiayias, Chair in Cyber Security and Privacy, School of Informatics, University of Edinburgh, interviewed by Nathan Jeffay, Edinburgh, Scotland, August 1, 2025.
2. M. M. A. A. M. Sony, M. B. Amin, A. Ashraf, K. M. A. Islam, N. C. Debnath, and G. C. Debnath, "Bias in AI-Driven HRM Systems: Investigating Discrimination Risks Embedded in AI Recruitment Tools and HR Analytics," *Social Sciences & Humanities Open* (2025), 12, 102082.
3. All Devarajan quotations: Harish Devarajan, interviewed by Nathan Jeffay, Ethereum Community Conference, Cannes, France, June 30, 2025.

Chapter 8: The Magic of Proofs

1. L. Babai, L. Fortnow, L. A. Levin, and M. Szegedy, "Checking Computations in Polylogarithmic Time," *Proceedings of the 23rd ACM Symposium on the Theory of Computing* (STOC 1991), pp. 21–31.
2. Two foundational papers introduced the PCP framework and its implications for complexity theory and approximation: S. Arora and S. Safra, "Probabilistic Checking of Proofs: A New

Characterization of NP," *Proceedings of the 33rd Annual Symposium on Foundations of Computer Science* (FOCS), IEEE, 1992, pp. 2–13; and S. Arora, C. Lund, R. Motwani, M. Sudan, and M. Szegedy, "Proof Verification and the Hardness of Approximation Problems," *Proceedings of the 33rd Annual Symposium on Foundations of Computer Science* (FOCS), IEEE, 1992, pp. 13–22.

Chapter 10: Blockchain in Practice: Usability, Scaling, and Privacy

1. S. Goldwasser, S. Micali, and C. Rackoff, "The Knowledge Complexity of Interactive Proof Systems," *SIAM Journal on Computing* (1989), 18(1), 186–208.
2. J. Gleick, "A New Approach to Protecting Secrets Is Discovered," *New York Times*, February 17, 1987.
3. O. Goldreich, S. Micali, and A. Wigderson, "Proofs that Yield Nothing But Their Validity," *Journal of the ACM*, 38(3), 1991 (conference version: FOCS 1986).
4. R. Gennaro, C. Gentry, B. Parno, and M. Raykova, "Quadratic Span Programs and Succinct NIZKs without PCPs," in Advances in Cryptology—EUROCRYPT 2013, Lecture Notes in Computer Science, vol. 7881 (Berlin, Heidelberg: Springer, 2013), 626–645.
5. E. Ben-Sasson, A. Chiesa, D. Genkin, E. Tromer, and M. Virza, "SNARKs for C: Verifying Program Executions Succinctly and in Zero Knowledge," in R. Canetti and Juan A. Garay (eds.), *Advances in Cryptology—CRYPTO 2013* (Lecture Notes in Computer Science), vol. 8043, pt. II, pp. 90–108.
6. I. Miers, C. Garman, M. Green, and A. D. Rubin, "Zerocoin: Anonymous Distributed E-Cash from Bitcoin," *Proceedings of the 2013 IEEE Symposium on Security and Privacy* (SP 2014), pp. 397–411.
7. E. Ben-Sasson, A. Chiesa, C. Garman, M. Green, I. Miers, E. Tromer, and M. Virza, "Zerocash: Decentralized Anonymous Payments from Bitcoin," *Proceedings of the 35th IEEE Symposium on Security and Privacy* (SP 2014), pp. 459–474.

Chapter 11: Research Springs to Life: From Breakthrough to Blueprint

1. Eli Ben-Sasson, Iddo Bentov, Yinon Horesh, and Michael Riabzev, "Scalable, Transparent, and Post-Quantum Secure Computational Integrity," Cryptology ePrint Archive, Paper 2018/046, 2018. This paper introduced the proof system now known as ZK-STARKs (Zero-Knowledge Scalable Transparent Arguments of Knowledge), emphasizing scalability, transparency (no trusted setup), and post-quantum security.

Chapter 12: StarkWare: From Genesis to $8 Billion

1. L. Goldberg, S. Papini, and M. Riabzev, "Cairo – a Turing-complete STARK-friendly CPU architecture," IACR Cryptology ePrint Archive, Report 2021/1063 (2021).
2. S. Nakamoto, "Bitcoin: A Peer-to-Peer Electronic Cash System" (2008). https://bitcoin.org/bitcoin.pdf.

Chapter 13: The Harshest Critique: Do We Even Need Crypto?

1. P. Krugman, "Bitcoin Is Evil," *The New York Times*, December 28, 2013. https://krugman.blogs.nytimes.com/2013/12/28/bitcoin-is-evil/.
2. P. Krugman, quoted in "No, Bitcoin Is Not Technobabble," *Cointelegraph*, June 7, 2021. https://cointelegraph.com/news/no-bitcoin-is-not-technobabble.
3. P. Krugman, "Transaction Costs and Tethers: Why I'm a Crypto Skeptic," *The New York Times*, July 31, 2018. https://www.nytimes.com/2018/07/31/opinion/transaction-costs-and-tethers-why-im-a-crypto-skeptic.html
4. C. Doctorow, "The 'Enshittification' of TikTok," *Wired*, January 21, 2023. https://www.wired.com/story/tiktok-platforms-cory-doctorow/.

Chapter 14: Stablecoins and Meme Coins

1. L. Ante, "From Adoption to Continuance: Stablecoins in Cross-border Remittances and the Role of Digital and Financial Literacy," *Telematics and Informatics* (2025), 97, 102230. https://doi.org/10.1016/j.tele.2024.102230. Findings reported by Blockchain Research Lab, February, 2025.
2. Statement from U.S. Secretary of the Treasury Scott Bessent on Enactment of the GENIUS Act, U.S. Department of the Treasury, July 18, 2025. https://home.treasury.gov/news/press-releases/sb0197.

Chapter 15: The Integrity Web

1. D. L. Hoffman, "Wanted: Net.Census," *Wired*, November 1, 1994. https://www.wired.com/1994/11/hoffman-if/.
2. Ibid.
3. S. Levy, "E-Money (That's What I Want)," *Wired*, December 1, 1994. https://www.wired.com/1994/12/emoney/.
4. *Dragons' Den*, "Hungryhouse Pitch," Series 5, November 19, 2007. https://www.youtube.com/watch?v=M4sJQxwpIqg.

Appendix: Questions About STARK Proofs Answered

1. The ideas underlying STARKs are based on many theoretical works in the field of computational complexity, too many to recount them all. Zero-knowledge proofs were introduced in the landmark paper of S. Goldwasser, S. Micali, and C. Rackoff, "The Knowledge Complexity of Interactive Proof Systems," *SIAM Journal on Computing* 18(1), 1989 (conference version: STOC 1985). Their applicability to all NP statements was established in O. Goldreich, S. Micali, and A. Wigderson, "Proofs that Yield Nothing But Their Validity," *Journal of the ACM*, 38(3), 1991 (conference version: FOCS 1986).

    The applications of validity proofs to succinct verification were first demonstrated in the pair of papers L. Babai, L. Fortnow, L. Levin, and M. Szegedy, "Checking Computations in Polylogarithmic Time," *SIAM Journal on Computing* 20(2), 1991 (conference version: STOC 1991) and L. Babai, L. Fortnow, and C. Lund, "Non-Deterministic Exponential Time Has Two-Prover Interactive

Protocols," (conference version: FOCS 1991) *Computational Complexity* 1(1), 1991, and L. Babai, L. Fortnow, C. Lund, and M. Szegedy, "Non-Deterministic Exponential Time Has Two-Prover Interactive Protocols," *Computational Complexity* 1, 1991 (conference version: FOCS 1991).The probabilistically checkable proofs (PCP) revolution is associated with the pair of publications S. Arora and S. Safra, "Probabilistic Checking of Proofs: A New Characterization of NP," *Journal of the ACM* 45(1), 1998, and S. Arora, C. Lund, R. Motwani, M. Sudan, and M. Szegedy, "Proof Verification and the Hardness of Approximation Problems," *Journal of the ACM* 45(3), 1998. These works received the Gödel Prize (2001).

Efficiency improvements critical to practical systems, so-called "quasi-linear PCPs" were developed in E. Ben-Sasson and M. Sudan, "Short PCPs with Polylog Query Complexity," *SIAM Journal on Computing* 38(2), 2008 (conference version: STOC 2005).The Fast Reed-Solomon IOP (FRI) protocol, which underlies the efficiency of modern STARKs, was introduced in E. Ben-Sasson, I. Bentov, Y. Horesh, and M. Riabzev, "Fast Reed–Solomon Interactive Oracle Proofs of Proximity," (conference version: ICALP 2018) and its most updated soundness analysis appeared in E. Ben-Sasson, D. Carmon, Y. Ishai, S. Kopparty and S. Saraf, "Proximity Gaps for Reed Solomon Codes," *Journal of the ACM* 70(5), 2023 (conference version: STOC 2020). The ZK STARK definitions and first construction appeared in E. Ben-Sasson, I. Bentov, Y. Horesh, and M. Riabzev, "Scalable, Transparent, and Post-Quantum Secure Computational Integrity," (conference version: CRYPTO 2018).

Acknowledgments

Several people made this book possible, and we want to thank them:

For help on the manuscript: John Jeffay and Josh O'Sullivan

For ideas: Katherine Kirkpatrick-Bos, Nitzan Shemer-Grossman, Harish Devarajan, and Gareth Jenkinson

For initiating and guiding the project: Philip Marino at Wiley. And for diligent editing, with flair, Angela Morrison

For support: Saul Hudson and Adrian Blust and his team at Tonal Media

For hospitality during research: the Abramson family

A Special Note from Eli

There would be many empty pages here were it not for the remarkable people of StarkWare who animate this story. First and foremost Uri Kolodny, StarkWare co-founder, board member, its first CEO, and my office mate for the first six years, my gratitude for decades of friendship, many bad dad jokes, and an occasional good one. Avihu Levy and Oren Katz from whom I learn daily and with whom I share my office and the duties of running StarkWare today. The amazing current and past giga-brains including Nevo Agmon, Abdelhamid Bakhta, Ohad Barta, Tom Brand, Dan Brownstein, Dan Carmon, Ittay Dror, Roei Engel, Oli Freuler, Lior Goldberg, Yuval Goldberg, Ulrich Haböck, Ran Grinshtein, Alex Gruell, Louis Guthman, Liron Hayman, Yonatan Iluz, Kheireddine Kamal, Gidi Kaempfer, Haim Krasniker, Rimon Labin, Ilya Lesokin, David Levit, Shahar Papini, Michael Riabzev, Kineret Segal, Shiri Teichman, Anat Veredgorn, Ilia Volokh, Ori Ziv—and all the others who work or who have worked in this extraordinary company.

The Starknet Foundation, still young and full of energy, is helping carry this adventure forward with leadership and vision, headed by

Acknowledgments

the clear-eyed James Strudwick and joined at the helm by Damian Chen, Jonathan Donald, Derek Flossman, Daniel Heyman, Henri Lieutaud, Bronwyn Long, and Ceri Power.

Also animating the story is the wider Starknet ecosystem and its StarkEx predecessor, full of contributors and numerous infrastructure and application developers, some known only by pseudonyms or NFT profile pictures, including Moody Salem (ekubo), Tarrence van As (Cartridge), Mentor Reka (AVNU), Apoorv Sadana (Karnot), Itamar Lesuisse and Julien Niset (Ready), Gabin Marignier (Focus Tree), Motty Lavie, Abraham Makovetsky, and Yoav Gaziel (Braavos), Federico Carrone (Lambda Class), Elias Tazartes and Clément Walter (Kakarot), LordOfAFew (Loot Realms), Loothero (Loot Survivor), Venkat Kunisetty (Endur.fi/Troves), Guilty Gyoza and Kunho Kim (Topology), Pierre Duperrin (Sorare), Ruslan Fakhrutdinov (Extended), Anand Gomes (Paradex), Will Harborne, Dan Yanev and Ross Middleton (Rhino.fi), Benjamin Flores (Starknet ID), Marcello Bardus and Kacper Koziol (Herodotus), Chris Lexmond (Influence), Sylvia Durach and Adam Borčány (Atomiq Labs), James and Robbie Ferguson and Alex Connolly (ImmutableX), Antonio Juliano (dYdX), Matteo Sanvido (Pragma), Nils Bundi (Vesu), Sean Han (Starkscan), Tomasz Stańczak and Jorik Schellekens (Nethermind), and many others.

We benefit from the encouragement and advice of many of the leaders of blockchain and related fields, including: Adam Back, Juan Benet, Arthur Breitman, Jeremy Bruestle, Joseph Chalom, Weiking Chen, Larry Cermak, Skaff Elias, Richard Garfield, Keith Grossman, Dan Held, Ethan Heilman, Matt Huang, Hong Kim, Georgios Konstantopoulos, Lev Livnev, Jack Liu, Joe Lubin, Mert Mumtaz, Charlie Noyes, Andrew Poelstra, Dan and Will Robinson, Jeremy Rubin, Kyle Samani, Balaji Srinivasan, Aubrey Strobel, Bobbin Threadbare, Paul Veradittakit, Eric Wall, and Anatoly Yakovenko.

Special thanks to Greg Maxwell and Mike Hearn, Bitcoin core developers who argued the advantages of ZK in blockchain early on. Zooko Wilcox-O'Hearn, Zcash co-founder and its first CEO, Naval Ravikant, startup guru with the smartest and crispest advice on any given topic, and Vitalik Buterin, Ethereum co-founder and long-time ZK-STARK enthusiast.

My journey started with mathematics, theoretical computer science, and computational complexity and I am forever grateful for

Acknowledgments

being exposed to this exciting field of knowledge and its brilliant leaders, including:

> Avi Wigderson, my PhD advisor and Optimus prime.
>
> Madhu Sudan, who introduced me to the complexity and beauty of probabilistically checkable proofs—the precursors of ZK-STARKs.
>
> Swastik Kopparty and Shubhangi Saraf, who created through their brilliant math a sound and everlasting foundation for STARKs.
>
> Noam Nisan, who taught me computational complexity as a young student, and Starknet tokenomics more recently.
>
> Shafi Goldwasser, whose work laid much of the foundation for zero-knowledge proofs and modern cryptography.

Over my academic career I had the pleasure of interacting with, and learning from, many students and postdocs. I formally advised some and informally worked with others. Many of them grew to be close collaborators and academic leaders, and also to impact my own path. Several even joined StarkWare and still work by my side. My gratitude to Iddo Bentov, Tom Brand (StarkWare Head of Product), Alessandro Chiesa (Zcash and StarkWare co-founder), Ariel Gabizon, Yinon Horesh, Yohay Kaplan, Michael Riabzev (StarkWare co-founder), Noga Ron Zewi, Alon Shtaierman (StarkWare Engineer) and Madars Virza (Zcash co-founder).

Last but by no means least from both the authors, love and thanks to our families:

> Ayelet Ben-Sasson and the Ben-Sasson children, and Tami Jeffay and the Jeffay children.

About the Authors

Eli Ben-Sasson is a mathematician and blockchain innovator. He helped to develop the mathematical theory that enables blockchain to serve a mass audience and was among the first to demonstrate that Zero Knowledge cryptography brings scale and privacy to blockchains. Eli is co-inventor of several foundational cryptographic protocols—STARK, FRI, and Zerocash. He was a co-founder and founding scientist of Zcash, and is co-founder, CEO, and Chairman of StarkWare. He sits on the board of the Starknet Foundation, the non-profit driving adoption of Starknet, a permissionless blockchain aiming to expand the Bitcoin economy. Eli has published dozens of peer-reviewed academic papers in the field of theoretical computer science, held research positions at the Institute for Advanced Study at Princeton, Harvard, MIT, and Technion, where he was a Professor of Computer Science. He is a married father of five. www.starkware.co/ceo

Nathan Jeffay is a journalist who fell into blockchain. He has covered geopolitics, wars, and the COVID-19 pandemic. Today Nathan works alongside Eli, telling the unfolding story of blockchain from the inside. As head of StarkWare's media desk, he focuses on explaining complex ideas clearly, honestly, and without hype. He is active in a range of projects for blockchain education, including podcasts, short movies, and news. Nathan is a married father of four. www.nathanoncrypto.com

Index

A

accountability
  of blockchain, 55
  of social media, 53–54
Africa, blockchain in, 85–86
AI. *See* artificial intelligence
algorithm, 50
  and AI systems, 2
  definition, 52
  emotion and, 53
  engagement-maximizing, 53
  gig economy and, 61
Alice and Bob, 22, 29
Ante, Lennart, 146, 147
Antonopoulos, Andreas M., 8
appeals, clear processes for, 56
Archimedes, 76, 78
Arora, Sanjeev, 75, 176
artificial intelligence (AI)
  accountability principle, 58
  compliance stamp, 59
  Human Resource Management and, 58–59
  Integrity Web, 156
  large language models, 59–60
  social media and, 57
  systems, algorithms, 2
  training data, 59
Augustus Gloop, 20
automated contract, 43–45

B

Babai, László, 75, 176
bank
  accounts, blockchain and, 83–84
  banking rails, 87

and traditional payment systems, 25
Bankman-Fried, Sam, 119
Bank of Cyprus, 32
Ben-Or, Michael, 95
Ben-Sasson, Eli, 7, 37, 38
Ben-Sasson–Sudan PCP of Proximity, 105, 106
Bentov, Iddo, 103, 107
Bessent, Scott, 149
Big Bang Theory, 28
Big Brother, 154, 160
Bitcoin (BTC), 7–8, 19–21, 32, 130, 138, 158
  avoids trusted setups, 101
  banks principles of, 138
  blockchain and, 24
  blocks, 12–13
  broadness, 10–11
  double-spend challenge, 29–30
  and Ethereum, 118
  exchange, 119
  genesis of, 9–10
  hard-coded cap, 31–32
  incentivized integrity, 13–15, 30–31
  internet money, 28
  money-only system, 9
  nodes, 11, 13
  prices, 3
  protocol rules, 11
  public verifiability, 11–12
  radical transparency, 23
  reversible payments, 33
  Satoshi Nakamoto, 28–29
  self-custody, 32–33
  Starknet, 131–132
  uses proof of work, 20

Bitcoin (BTC) (*Continued*)
  validity proofs and, 73
  Zcash and, 19–21
  zero-knowledge proofs and, 99
Bitcoin conference (2013), 7, 71, 72, 78, 90
Bitcoin Magazine, 114
BitTorrent, 68
Block 0 Bitcoin, 10
blockchain, xiii, 81
  in Africa, 85–86
  artificial intelligence and, 57–60
  automated contract, 43–45
  bank accounts and, 83–84
  Bitcoin and, 24, 138
    blocks, 12–13
    broadness, 10–11
    genesis of, 9–10
    incentivized integrity, 13–15
    money-only system, 9
    nodes, 11, 13
    protocol rules, 11
    public verifiability, 11–12
  blocks, 12–13
    consensus mechanism ensures, 18
    fingerprint features, 21–22
    and proposes, 20
  broadness, 153
  building, applications, 27
  Cairo, 124
  computation off, 169–170
  as concrete tool, 84
  consensus protocol, 18
  coordinating at scale (human beings and human society), 1, 4–5
  core principles, scaling without abandoning, 73
  cross-border online labor market, 86
  crypto, 135–139
  and cryptographic guarantees, 55
  definition, 17
  as digital tool, 84–85
  documents and data, 1, 2, 4–5
  as enabler, 62–63
  Ethereum, 33–36
  fingerprint features, 21–22
  fragility records, 40–43
  game developers, 150
  general-purpose, 40, 44
  gig economy and, 60–62
  incentivized integrity, 153
  infrastructure, 37–47
  Integrity Web, 151–153
    emerging, 157–158
    human dignity, 154–155
    idealism of, 158–159
    infrastructure, 156–157
    owning your life, 159–161
    Starknet, 157–158, 161–162
  mass adoption, 45–47
  meme coin
    Dogecoin, 144–145
    and stablecoins, 145
  multi-threaded, 131
  openness, 131
  operating system, 138
  own your life and, 56, 57
  participation, 19
  perpetual futures, 150
  prediction markets, 150
  privacy concerns, 22–24
  privacy-preserving mechanisms, 89
  public or permissioned, 17–18
  public verifiability, 153
  radical transparency, 23–25
  rails, 87
  reach consensus, 20–21
  roadblocks to adoption, 65–69
  scalability, 71, 89, 131
  smart contract, 22
  social media apps and, 54
    clear processes for appeals, 56
    identity verification, 55–56

Index

permanence and accountability, 55
system-level rights can't be rewritten, 56
transparent decision-making, 55
speed, 131
stablecoins
  adoption, 147–148
  GENIUS Act, 148–149
  and meme coins, 145
  remittances, 146–147
Starknet, 129–131
and STARK proofs, 165
technology, 1–2
  IntegrityLand, 3–4
  protects "stuff," 4–6
traditional databases, 41–42
and zero-knowledge proofs, 156
The Boy Who Harnessed the Wind (movie), 84
Breitman, Arthur, 114
broadcasting, 98
broadness
  Bitcoin, 10–11, 15
  resonate, radical transparency and, 24–25
BTC. *See* Bitcoin
Buterin, Vitalik, 34, 114, 115
Byron, Andy, 53

C

Cairo (programming language), 123–124
Carmon, Dan, 107
Casares, Wences, 47
Cattelan, Maurizio, 145
centralized exchanges (CEXs), 119, 121
Charlie and the Chocolate Factory, 20, 175
ChatGPT, 59–60
Chiesa, Alessandro, 96
Circle (USD), 148

cloud computing, 2
Cloudflare, 138
Coatue, 125
"code is law," 20
Coinbase, 124
CoinDesk, 125
Comedian (Cattelan), 145
complexity class. *See* nondeterministic polynomial time
computation, 74, 165
  checking, 75–76
  class of, 172
  off the blockchain, 169–170
  and STARKs, 166
consensus protocol
  blockchain, 18, 20
C programming language, 97
cross-border transaction, 143–144
crypto, 87
  and blockchain, 136–139
  critiques of, 135–136
  traditional, 66–67
  usability problem, 66
crypto-backed debit card, 87–88
cryptocurrency, 22, 23, 39, 66, 67
cryptographic proofs, xiii, 170
cryptography, 7, 22, 23, 35, 93, 174
CryptoKitties, 68
CUDA, 123, 124
"cult" (Bitcoin), 136
Cybersecurity conference (2017), 113
cypherpunks, 7

D

Darth Vader, 101, 111, 127
databases, traditional, 41
decentralization-security-scalability trilemma, 68, 89
decentralized exchange (DEX), 119–121
Devarajan, Harish, 61, 62
DEX. *See* decentralized exchange

digital fingerprint, 174
Digital Gold, 32
digital presence, of company, 55
digital space, 51, 127, 160, 161
Doctorow, Cory, 137
Dogecoin, 144–145
DoorDash, 61, 62
double-spend challenge, 29–30
Dragons' Den (Shark Tank), 152
dYdX, 121

E

Edison, Thomas, xi
Ehrsam, Fred, 124
elliptic-curve-based systems, 109
elliptic-curve cryptography (ECC), 96, 101
enabler, blockchain as, 62–63
engagement, 52–53
enshittification, 137
error-correcting codes, 168
ETHCC. *See* Ethereum Community Conference
Ethereum, 19, 21, 115, 130, 158
  and Bitcoin, 118
  conceptual leap to, 33–36
  conferences, 37, 38
  model, 39–40
  neutral settlement layer, 35
  smart contract, 44–45
  StarkEx, 121, 127
  Starknet, 131
  yellow paper, 34
Ethereum Community Conference (ETHCC), 37, 61
Ethereum Foundation, 107

F

Facebook, 52, 53, 153
Fast Fourier Transform (FFT), 104, 107
Fast Reed-Solomon IOP (FRI) protocol, 176
Fast RS IOP (FRI) protocol, 111, 176
  breakthrough, 105–107
Fermat's Last Theorem, 73, 90, 92
FFT. *See* Fast Fourier Transform
financial crash (2008), 139
financial crisis (2001), 32
financial system, crumbling, 46
fingerprint features, 21–22
Forbes, 125
Fortnow, Lance, 75, 176
fragility of records, 40–43
Freedom of Information, 11
FRI protocol. *See* Fast Reed-Solomon IOP protocol
FTX exchange, 119
funding round, 115

G

galactic algorithms, 95, 106
Garman, Christina, 97
"gas fees," 67, 121
genesis block (Block 0), 10
Genius Act (2025), 163
GENIUS Act. *See* Guaranteed Electronic Nationwide Infrastructure for Ubiquitous Stablecoins
Genkin, Daniel, 96
Gennaro, Rosario, 96
Gentry, Craig, 96
GGPR construction, ZK-SNARK system, 96
gig economy, blockchain and, 60–62
gig workers, 83–84
Gitcoin Grants, 160
Gleick, James, 94
global Ethereum community, 37
global financial crisis (2009), 10
global remittance corridors, 86–88
Goldberg, Lior, 117, 123
Goldreich, Oded, 176
Goldwasser, Shafi, 93, 94, 176

Google's Gemini, 60
GPUs, 123, 124
Greek kryptós, 7
Green, Matt, 97
Greenoaks Capital, 125
Grubhub, 61, 62
Guaranteed Electronic Nationwide Infrastructure for Ubiquitous Stablecoins (GENIUS Act), 148

H
"halting problem," 76
hard-coded cap Bitcoin, 32
Hashdex, 45
Haun, Katie, 114
Hileman, Garrick, 8
Horesh, Yinon, 103, 107
human dignity demands, 154
Human Resource Management (HRM), AI and, 58–59
Hume, David, 51–52
Hungryhouse, 152

I
ICO. *See* initial coin offering
identity verification, blockchain, 55–56
incentivized integrity, 12–15, 30–31, 138
initial coin offering (ICO), 114
Instagram, 52, 53
integrity
  incentives and, 22–23
  and STARKs proofs, 177
IntegrityLand, 3–4
Integrity Web, xiii, 42, 43, 151–153
  emerging, 157–158
  human dignity, 154–155
  idealism of, 158–159
  infrastructure, 156–157
  owning your life, 159–161
  Starknet, 157–158, 161–162
Interactive Oracle Proofs (IOPs), 176

interactive proofs (IP), 72
  and zero-knowledge proofs, 176
internet, 49
  blockchain and, xiii, 86
  as digital native, xi
  money, xi, xiii, 28
IOPs. *See* Interactive Oracle Proofs
Ishai, Yuval, 107

J
Jeffay, Nathan, 1, 17, 19, 36, 40, 114, 156

K
Kaempfer, Gideon, 117
Katz, Oren, 117
Kiayias, Aggelos, 51, 57–59, 156
Kirkpatrick Bos, Katherine, 23
"kiss cam scandal," 52–53
Kolodny, Uri, 113–115, 117, 118
Kopparty, Swastik, 107
Krugman, Paul, 135, 136

L
large language models (LLMs), 59–60
layer 1 (L1) blockchain, 121
layer 2 (L2) blockchain, 26, 121
ledger, 10
  bank's electronic, 4
  shared digital, 1, 9
  tamper-proof public, 5
Lesuisse, Itamar, 158
Levin, Leonid A., 75, 176
Levy, Avihu, 117, 118
Lewis, C. S., 6
light client, 72
line-shaft systems, xi
Lipton, Richard, 95
LLMs. *See* large language models
low-degree polynomial (mathematical rule), 106
Lund, Carsten, 75, 176

M

Magri, Bernardo, 45–46
mass adoption, 45–47
mathematical proofs, xiii, 73–74
mathematics, power of, 115
Matt Huang, 124
Maxwell, Greg, 73
Meaden, Deborah, 152
meme coin
    Dogecoin, 144–145
    and stablecoins, 145
Merkle tree blockchain, 174
Micali, Silvio, 93, 94, 176
Miers, Ian, 97
miners, 12, 19, 20, 30–31
mining, 14
moon math, 126
Motwani, Rajeev, 75, 176
"multi-threaded" blockchain economy, 131
Musk, Elon, 145

N

Nakamoto, Satoshi, 10, 28, 29, 131–132
Naor, Moni, 108
NASCAR, 145
Nasdaq, 129
"A New Approach to Protecting Secrets" (article), 93
Newsweek (magazine), 28
The New York Times, 135
NEXP. *See* nondeterministic exponential time
NFT. *See* non-fungible token
Niset, Julien, 158
nodes
    Bitcoin, 11, 13
    form network of computers, 19
    in network checks, 30
nondeterministic exponential time (NEXP), 172
nondeterministic polynomial time (NP), 176

non-fungible token (NFT), 45
NP. *See* nondeterministic polynomial time
NVIDIA, 123, 124

O

"on-chain" app, 69
open-ended software, 40
openness, in blockchain, 131
Operation Legacy, 43
opportunity, blockchain, 131

P

P2P. *See* peer-to-peer
pandemic, 160
Pantera VCs, 118
Papini, Shahar, 123
Paradigm, 118, 124
Parno, Bryan, 96
PCPs. *See* probabilistically checkable proofs
peer-to-peer (P2P), 18, 144
Peppa Pig, 111
permanence, of blockchain, 55
permissioned blockchains, 18
perpetual futures cases, 150
PoC. *See* proof of concept
Polygon, 103
Polymarket, 150
Ponzi scheme, 136
PoS. *See* proof-of-stake
post-quantum secure (safe even from future quantum computers), 176
PoW. *See* proof-of-work
prediction markets cases, 150
privacy, 25
    blockchain, 131
    STARKs proofs, 168–169, 177
    zero-knowledge, 90–91
privacy-preserving technologies, 23
private blockchains, 18
private businesses, 40

probabilistically checkable proofs (PCPs), 72, 96, 101, 104–106, 176
proof of concept (PoC), 119
proof-of-stake (PoS) systems, 19, 21
proof-of-work (PoW), 20, 30
prover, 170–171
  interaction, 106
    validity proofs, 74, 77–78, 80
    zero-knowledge proofs and, 92–93
proximity testing, 106
public blockchain, 17–18
public verifiability, 11, 15
Pythagoreans, 75

Q

quality broadness, 10–11
quantum computers, 174–175

R

Rackoff, Charles, 93, 94, 176
radical transparency, 11–12, 23, 27, 138
  and broadness resonate, 24–25
Raykova, Mariana, 96
records, fragility of, 40–43
Reed-Solomon codes, 168
Regan, Ken, 95
regulation, as roadblock to blockchain, 66
Reuters, 125
revenue, advertising, 53
Riabzev, Michael, 103, 107, 123
RiscZero, 103
roadblocks to blockchain, 65–66
  regulation, 66
  scaling (or tricky) trilemma, 67–69
  user experience, 66–67
RSA accumulators, 97

S

Safra, Muli, 75, 176
San Jose Convention Center, 7

Saraf, Shubhangi, 107
scalability, 68, 71, 129, 168
scalable (handles massive computations), 176
"Scalable, Transparent, and Post-Quantum Secure Computational Integrity" (paper), 103
Scalable Transparent ARguments of Knowledge. *See* STARK
scale, in blockchain, 131
scaling trilemma, 67–69, 72, 89
security, scaling trilemma, 68
seed round, 124
  funding, 115
Segev, Gil, 108
self-custody, 66
Sequoia Capital, 125
Series B round, 124
Series C round, 124–125
Series D round, 125
shared digital ledger, 1, 9
Sheldon Cooper, 28
Shiba Inu, 144
shielded addresses, Zcash, 99
slashing, 21
smart contract, 22, 43, 127
  blockchain-based, 44
  execution environment for, 35
Smith, Adam, 51
SNARK, 98
"SNARKs for C," (paper), 96–97
social media, 50
  accountability of, 53–54
  advertisers, 53
  apps, blockchain and, 54–57
  companies, 50–51, 54
  platforms, 53
  unsettling setup of, 51
Solana, 158
Sorare, 121
soundness
  cryptographic system, 175
  error, 106

speed
  in blockchain, 131
  and STARKs proofs, 173, 174, 177
Srinivasan, Balaji, 119
stablecoins, 87, 141–144
  adoption, 147–148
  GENIUS Act, 148–149
  and meme coins, 145
  remittances, 146–147
stake (collateral), 19, 21
"stake" validators, 21
standard mathematical tools, 109
STARK, xiii, xiv, 25, 78, 154, 157
  breakthrough, 103–105
  discovering, 100–102
  FRI protocol, 105–107, 111
  proofs
    analogy maps to actual
      machinery, 167
    Bit Deeper, delving, 167–168
    and blockchains, 165, 177
    computation, 165–166
    creating a, 172
    cryptography, 174–175
    ideas of, 176–177
    nondeterministic
      exponential time, 172
    privacy, 168–169
    prover (worker bee), 170–171
    against quantum
      computers, 174–175
    Reed-Solomon codes, 168
    soundness, 175
    verification speed, 173–174
    verifiers (checker), 171
    zero knowledge, 169
  theory to infrastructure, 112
STARK (paper), 108–109,
  113, 114
STARK-based networks, 121
StarkEx, 120–121, 126–127, 177
Starknet, 15, 19, 21, 35, 122,
  123, 175, 177
  launching, 126–128

StarkWare, 35, 38, 61, 78, 102,
  103, 117, 157
  in Africa, 85
  Bitcoin, 131–133
  blockchain, 129–131
  Cairo (programming
    language), 123–124
  first proof, 118
  founding of, 114–115
  infrastructure, 122–123
  investment and
    valuation, 124–125
  launch of Starknet, 126–128
  market momentum, 118–119
  STARKs enforce custody,
    119–120
  used STARKs, 112
Succinct, 103
succinct validity proofs, 80–81
succinct verification, 96
  in computer science, 76
  definition, 74
  importance, in 2013, 80–81
  and scale, 73–75
  working of, 79–80
Sudan, Madhu, 75, 104–106, 176
supercomputers, 75–76, 110
system-level rights, blockchain, 56
Szegedy, Mario, 75, 176

T

tamper-proof public ledger, 5
TechCrunch, 125
Technion's cybersecurity
  center, 113–114
"technobabble" (crypto), 136
Telematics and Informatics
  (journal), 146
temporary fork, 21
Tether (USD), 148
Tiger Global, 125
TikTok, 53, 160
The Times of London, 10
$T \times \log(T)$ formula, 172–174

top-tier VCs, 124
traditional finance (TradFi), 142
transparent (no hidden keys or trusted setup), 176
transparent decision-making, blockchain, 55
trivia quizmaster, xiii
Tromer, Eran, 96
Turing, Alan, 76

U
Uber, 61
Unchained podcast, 47
Unified Payments Interface (UPI), 143
United States, 41, 47, 137, 148
  Genius Act (2025) in, 163
United States Dollar Coin (USDC), 141, 143
United States Dollar Tether (USDT), 141, 146
UPI. *See* Unified Payments Interface
USDC. *See* United States Dollar Coin
US dollar stablecoin, 141, 142, 144
USDT. *See* United States Dollar Tether
user experience, as roadblock to blockchain, 66–67
U.S. Treasuries, 148–149

V
validators (block producers), 19
validity proofs, 71, 78
  Bitcoin and, 73
  feeling of excitement, 76
  galactic algorithms, 95
  integrity, 78–79
  privacy, 90
  prover, 74, 77–78, 80
  scale, 90
  verifier and, 74, 75, 77–78, 80
Van Valkenburgh, Peter, 114
verifier, 171

interaction, 106
validity proofs, 74, 75, 77–78, 80
zero-knowledge proofs and, 92–93
virtuous cycle, stablecoin, 147
Virza, Madars, 96
Volokh, Ilia, 156
Voorhees, Erik, 8

W
Wigderson, Avi, 94, 176
Wilcox O'Hearn, Zooko, 98–99, 114
Wiles, Andrew, 73, 90–91
William Kamkwamba, 84
Wired (article), 151
World Bank, 146
world-changing technology, xi
Wright, Craig, 28

X
X (formerly Twitter), 52
  Grok, 60
Xapo Bank, 47

Y
YouTube, 52, 53, 160

Z
Zcash, 15, 23, 114, 130, 158
  and Bitcoin, 19–21
  blockchains, 35
  "Ceremony" (2016), 99
  as cryptocurrency, 99
  cryptographic protocol, 23
  SNARKs used in, 101
  ZEC price spike, 100
  Zerocash protocol, 98
  ZK-SNARKs and, 105
ZEC (coin of Zcash network), 100
"Zerocash" (paper), 97
Zerocash protocol, 97–98, 100

"Zerocoin" (paper), 97
zero-knowledge blockchain
        systems, 58
zero-knowledge proof (ZK proof),
        12, 23, 25, 72, 73, 89, 107,
        169, 171, 175
    and blockchains, 156
    Cairo, 124
    combination lock example, 91–92
    from controversy to
        acceptance, 93–95
    definition, 91
    for general-purpose
        computation, 97–98
    interactive proofs and, 176
    properties, 94
    prover, 92–93
    usage of, 91
    verifier, 92–93
    working of, 91–93
zero-knowledge technology, 58
ZK cryptography, 34
ZK-SNARKs, 23, 25, 96, 105, 109
    Achilles' heel, 109–110
    GPR construction of, 96
    for privacy applications, 97
    trusted setup for, 99–100
    Zerocash protocol, 97–98
ZK-STARKs, 101, 126, 175
    math of, 120
    and StarkEx, 121
zkSync, 103